What peopl

In STEP with

Margaret Fell, wife of George Fox, is celebrated as the "mother of Quakerism" but her profound and original spirituality has been all but lost. Joanna Godfrey Wood's appropriate "bringing to new light" of the essence of Fell's central texts is a major Quaker re-discovery. Her examination of Fell's explorations of the four great spiritual STEPs through the concepts of Simplicity, Truth, Equality and Peace has been a personal pilgrimage that can now be ours. Her research unearths fresh meaning through adaptations of Fell's language, enriched by a series of ideas and notes, which together give a contemporary relevance to her historic experience.

Alec Davison, a founder of The Leaveners, Quaker Quest and The Kindlers

In this inspiring and beautiful book Joanna creates a bridge across time to the writings of Margaret Fell over 350 years ago. The personal experiences and reflections of these two women are woven together as we share their journeys of discovery. A reminder of the roots of Quakerism. A joy to travel with them both.

Ruth Tod, author of *Positive Parenting for a Peaceful World*

This is a fascinating book, a unique blend of reminiscence, commentary and Quaker wisdom. Joanna Godfrey Wood is an expert guide to the work of Margaret Fell, a lynch-pin of the early Quaker movement in Britain. She uses well-chosen extracts from Fell's writing to shed light not only on the beginnings of Quakerism, but on the lives of Quakers today – in particular their commitment to simplicity, truth, equality and peace. Her book is accessible, thought-provoking and exhilarating; invaluable to seasoned Quakers and essential reading for anyone interested in the ways in which Quakers find meaning and purpose.

Geoffrey Durham, author of *What Do Quakers Believe?*, *Being a Quaker: A Guide for Newcomers* and *The Spirit of the Quakers*

An agreeable, thorough and truthful exploration of how it is to be a Quaker today. Joanna pulls no punches in offering challenges that we, as Quakers, need to shine Light on. Going back to Margaret Fell's writings and bringing them into modern parlance within our present Testimonies provides a very good anchorage for first-time spiritual explorers finding paths to shine the Light within. This is where we can find our power and take small steps towards dealing with inner and outer callings. As both Margaret Fell and Joanna Godfrey Wood say, albeit with a 350-year gap and a very different language style, the content remains the same: within the darkness is the Light. Be brave, be courageous, have faith, but "go there."

Isa Louise Levy, MA, artist and arts psychotherapist

Joanna Godfrey Wood, driven to understand her lifelong faith more deeply, and seeking that force of Truth "that first brought Quakerism into being," has turned to the "unread Fell." There she has found a true friend and sure guide, and it is a faithfulness to Fell's animating spirit that she has shared with us the fruits of this encounter.

Thom Bonneville, member of North-West London Area Meeting

QUAKER QUICKS

In STEP with Quaker Testimony

Simplicity, Truth, Equality and Peace –
inspired by Margaret Fell's writings

QUAKER QUICKS

In STEP with Quaker Testimony

Simplicity, Truth, Equality and Peace – inspired by Margaret Fell's writings

Joanna Godfrey Wood

CHRISTIAN ALTERNATIVE
BOOKS

Winchester, UK
Washington, USA

JOHN HUNT PUBLISHING

First published by Christian Alternative Books, 2021
Christian Alternative Books is an imprint of John Hunt Publishing Ltd.,
No. 3 East St., Alresford, Hampshire SO24 9EE, UK
office@jhpbooks.com
www.johnhuntpublishing.com
www.christian-alternative.com

For distributor details and how to order please visit the 'Ordering' section on our website.

ISBN: 978 1 78904 577 2
978 1 78904 578 9 (ebook)
Library of Congress Control Number: 2020930844

A CIP catalogue record for this book is available from the British Library.

Design: Stuart Davies

UK: Printed and bound by CPI Group (UK) Ltd, Croydon, CR0 4YY
Printed in North America by CPI GPS partners

We operate a distinctive and ethical publishing philosophy in
all areas of our business, from our global network of authors to
production and worldwide distribution.

Contents

Also by this author

Travelling in the Light
How Margaret Fell's writings can speak to Quakers today
978-0-9933627-6-7

In Search of Stillness
Using a simple meditation to find inner peace
978-1-78904-707-3

Turn to the Light which cometh from the Father of Lights which draws your minds towards God and let this be your Teacher and Leader.
Margaret Fell

Foreword

About Margaret Fell

Margaret Fell (1614–1702), one of the first Quakers and certainly the best-known female Friend from the era of early Quakerism, has long been affectionately called the "mother of Quakerism," though some now feel that this is to patronize her. She was certainly motherly in terms of being a welcoming hostess, opening up her home to visiting itinerant seekers and preachers, who were common in this time of ferment during the English Civil War. Her well-established household became a vital hub for the establishment of the early Quaker movement – and they say that the food was very good. But she is far more significant for early Quakerism than she has been given credit for. She wrote a vast collection of vital campaigning and theological work, which has not been kept in print, has been poorly acknowledged, even forgotten, even though it seems that she may have been responsible for some of the key Quaker findings in the early days of seeking.

Some of her writing about the "Light," especially, as well as her other thoughts and ideas, are similar to George Fox's, the well-known and amply acknowledged co-founder of the Quaker movement. But does she have something to say in her own right? Is it slightly different from what Fox had to say? And has she been passed over? Do we need to take more notice of what she has to say and go back to her writings now?

Fell was born in 1614, was married firstly to Judge Thomas Fell (1632) and secondly, following Judge Fell's death, to George Fox (born 1624). Fox was one of the most well-known founders of Quakerism in the mid-seventeenth century. Between 1633 and 1653 Fell and Judge Fell had eight children and Margaret ran a large household and estate at Swarthmoor, Ulverston, England, often single-handed, at a time of enormous religious and social crisis, both physical and spiritual. The country was torn apart by civil war, which broke out in 1642. Many died and were imprisoned, and great long-lasting changes occurred in society at that time. Fell endured long imprisonments and suffered greatly for her faith and actions, which included campaigning, traveling in ministry and holding meetings at her home. She died in 1702, aged 88.

Acknowledgments

Special thanks to Isa Louise Levy of Muswell Hill Meeting, North-West London Area Meeting, London, UK, for mentoring me through the writing process and providing crucial feedback. Grateful thanks also to Ruth Tod for her invaluable comments.

Thanks to all members of Muswell Hill Meeting, particularly those involved in the study group in 2019 which explored some of the writings of Margaret Fell using an early draft of *Travelling in the Light: How Margaret Fell's writings can speak to Quakers today*, Joanna Godfrey Wood, The Kindlers, 2019.

Thanks to all those involved in the Equipping for Ministry course 2017–19, Woodbrooke Quaker Study Centre, Birmingham, England, and particularly Stuart Masters and Betty Hagglund.

Introduction

About Quakers

Quakers (the Religious Society of Friends) are a Christian-based sect originating in England and now found worldwide. The unprogrammed tradition is the style of meeting for worship followed in the UK, Europe, Australia and New Zealand and in the US (where several different forms of Quakerism are practiced). Unprogrammed worship involves waiting, as a group, without a minister or pastor, in silence and stillness, in which there is no pre-planned ministry or order of service, though members may feel led to speak, or "minister." Quakers following other, semi-programmed and programmed formats for meetings for worship, which may include pre-planned ministry, are found in high numbers in the United States, Africa and South America, as well as in other countries. Such meetings, which developed at a later time than the unprogrammed versions, usually have appointed leaders or pastors.

Unprogrammed Quakers usually meet for worship weekly on a Sunday, but at other times too, waiting in silence and searching within. Spirit-led action may result, including unplanned vocal ministry, perhaps sometimes involving, or supplemented by, reading from Quaker literature and the Bible. Christianity is in the roots and origins of Quakerism and many Friends identify as Christian, though many today do not. Both approaches are considered equally "Quaker."

Creed or no creed?

Quakers do not have a creed, as such, though they do have what could be called broad guidelines, which we look at in this book: Simplicity, Truth, Equality and Peace. These are core words, though others are included according to preference. Generally, Quakers search inwardly for guidance under the workings of the "other," "Spirit" or "God." In unprogrammed Quakerism there is no formal intermediary between the group or individual and the power that many call "God," so "beliefs" are not a fixed understanding or requirement. Gradually a "way" to live by is formed through individual discernment and discovery, in meeting and in life generally, and in personal experience. It is recognized that such discoveries might have common ground but may be very different too, because we are all individuals and experiences, understandings and interpretations vary.

The nature of ministry

"Ministry" may or may not occur in the unprogrammed tradition, but when it does it comes from a deep place, prompted by "other" or "Spirit," or that which may be called "God." The adrenaline kick experienced when someone is suddenly prompted to stand in the silent meeting and starts to speak from a place of encountered Truth may produce a physical shaking, stammering and hesitation, a hammering of the heart. This phenomenon, often evident to others, originally brought about the nickname "Quaker." This started as a mockery but it has now stuck. Spoken ministry in meeting is not a carefully prepared, rounded speech, but more of a gradual exploration and unfolding of the experience of Truth. It may be very brief. Others in the meeting may take up a theme to explore more deeply, after a period of further silence, or they may speak about something seemingly unrelated. Ministry emerges from silence and stillness. There is no discussion, answering or debating. The piece of ministry may be meaningful for some but others may not hear or want its message – or its significance may come to them later. Alternatively, there may be unbroken quiet.

In a broader sense "ministry" might also take the form of promptings to act in the wider world, which might include, for example, undertaking practical tasks or "acting under a concern" in a campaigning capacity. This is a very personal thing and those who act usually feel urged from a place that seems to be "other" than, and separate from, their own thoughts, will or decision-making process.

How this book came about

The question "Why am I a Quaker?" was at the forefront of my mind when I started to look into the roots and origins of Quakerism. How does my life in Quakerism today connect with Margaret Fell's in the seventeenth century? Where do our modern Quaker testimonies, Simplicity, Truth, Equality and Peace, come from and can we find first glimpses of them in early Quaker writings, such as Fell's? This book attempts to recapture some of the things I discovered one winter when I sat down to transcribe a long volume of Margaret Fell's writings (*A Brief Collection of Remarkable Passages* ...), published in 1710, but not re-issued since. As I struggled to read and type from an old and precious book placed delicately on a cushion, the words passed through my center and I found that I could "hear" Fell's voice speaking to me loudly and clearly. I realized that this process, though arduous and undertaken with the intention of eventually republishing Fell's work, was an effective way of reading it and thinking about it. The repetitive, automatic action of typing freed up my brain to absorb the words in a way that ordinary reading would not have done. My fingers kept me focused and this led me to thinking about creativity and the ways in which physical activity can release it.

As I ploughed through Fell's book, I thought about the laboriousness of writing and printing by hand in the seventeenth century, compared with speedy modern writing, editing and printing processes. I thought about J. Sowle, the printer, and his daughter, who in 1710 printed and published the original, slaving over tiny separate slivers of type – the same process used until the advent of computer typesetting. I found some mistakes in their painstaking work that allowed me to connect with them as fallible human beings. I discovered a few things about Fell and about Quakerism that I had long forgotten or ignored – or had failed to be aware of in the first place. These things came at a perfect time. They were revelatory and allowed me to re-kindle some ideas about Quakerism that I had been missing for a long time but without fully realizing it.

STEP as a structure

This book uses Fell's writings and adaptations of them as starting off points for thoughts about Quakerism, beginning with the words Simplicity, Truth, Equality and Peace. My thoughts, divided into themes, are meanderings; they do not always follow a steady path. It is hoped that this book provides inspiration for others and discussion points for Quaker groups.

What made early Quakers work so fiercely and steadfastly to establish Quakerism in the mid-seventeenth century? What had they discovered? How were their discoveries different from the religion of the time and why were they important? How can we rediscover these things for ourselves today?

Early Quaker thinking was rooted firmly and confidently in the King James Bible, which was widely read in ordinary homes as soon as more people became literate – and it helped people to become literate. Daily Bible reading was part of the fabric of family life and many knew long passages by heart. Margaret Fell exhorted all to read the Bible and search for Truth in it and her use of it in her writings reveals deep understanding.

In some homes births, marriages and deaths were recorded on the flyleaves of large-format Bibles and the family Bible was an important part of hearth and home and family life. I am fortunate to own one such volume. It is so big that is almost a piece of furniture in its own right and so old that it has to be held together with straps and buckles. It is really a mound of dust waiting to happen. The pages speak of hours, days, months and years of loyal family devotion and the flyleaf records a huge number of children born into that family, all in order of birth.

Early Quakers made discoveries in the Bible that they felt had been missed, ignored or interpreted wrongly by the established church. They found that the word Truth most closely embodied their beliefs and named themselves "Friends of Truth" initially. In later centuries "precepts" or "testimonies" were identified and listed as separate "Quaker words" that are closely connected and overlapping. In Britain Yearly Meeting these are presently Simplicity, Truth, Equality and Peace (STEP), but more words are being added as time goes by and they vary in different yearly meetings around the world. Words may have been dropped or incorporated into one of the other categories. Perhaps Integrity is part of Truth, though we might today wonder why this quality should be particular to Quakers, or why Peace should be either – or indeed any of them. They are all ideas being explored by other religious bodies and peoples worldwide and perhaps it is not for the Society of Friends to claim ownership, if this is so. So do these separate words and their various additions (such as Community and Sustainability) help or hinder our understanding and practice of Quakerism? They are all so intertwined that you soon find that you cannot have one without the other and there is much overlapping. In addition, there are different ways in which the ideas can be combined to work together in one's mind. For example, you could say that the Equality of all beings is a Simple Truth, which begins in Peace and leads to it too. Or Peace is found in the Simplicity of stillness, where all are Equal under Truth. Or stillness is a Simple Truth where all can find Equality and Peace. One idea feeds into another – and back again. None stands alone. But ultimately, what we are talking about, perhaps, is Truth. Simplicity leads to Truth, Equality leads to Truth and Peace leads to Truth and Truth, in turn, leads to all of these.

So I have structured the book around the four main modern Quaker Testimonies, taking a broad view of them, and have tried to see whether they, or the ideas that formed them, are found in Fell's writings. The words are certainly there, but meanings have changed or are used differently and we need to explore whether the ideas of Simplicity, Truth, Equality and Peace were really there, as we think of them and understand them today, or whether we have overlaid the words with different meanings as well as new layers of complexity, which perhaps were not intended. Perhaps the birthing of the ideas was present, but in a simpler, more everyday, form. The ideas grew and expanded from these beginnings.

As they are now presented in modern Quaker literature the Testimonies seem more intertwined than ever, even though they were separated under distinct headings to make them more understandable and perhaps more useable. However, I am not convinced that isolating ideas really serves us today, as it seems that Peace, for example, is the one that some inquirers are drawn to, but find, often with some disappointment, that this is only part of the Quaker message. I have met new inquirers who are under impression that Quakers are nothing to do with religion, but rather a meditation group working for peace and doing "good works." In the wider world, which seems quite badly fractured, perhaps we need instead to draw the strands of testimony together to gain a greater sense of wholeness and of being connected, joined up, rather than maintaining discrete ideas, which may over-simplify and fail to serve as they should. Perhaps we need to find a greater sense of "everything having an impact on everything else" and feel that it might be a mistake to isolate ideas, for fear of losing their connectedness.

The roots of the Testimonies in Fell's writings

The words Simplicity, Truth, Equality and Peace are used differently in Fell's writings than our modern headings may imply today. Sometimes they only hint at the concept as we think of it now, and it seems to be there in the background rather than part of the main thought or argument. For example, "equal" and "equality" are ideas that Fell seems to take as a given – perhaps well understood by Friends at the time. All people are equal in God's vision and kingdom. Equality is not referred to often, but when it is it jolts one awake. There is a split second of recognition. It seems to hint at the foundations rather than the building itself. The same is true of "peace." The word does not occur often in Fell's writings, and it refers to the state of inner peace rather than anything outward or concerned with "war." The word "truth" comes up frequently and is a major theme at the core of Fell's thought and life. It is the central Quaker tenet – then and now. Perhaps we could think of this as being our main Testimony and pull all the others together within it.

"God" and "that of God"

There is no general agreement, within modern unprogrammed Quakerism, about what "God" is, or even, these days, whether it is an assumed part of the Society of Friends. Perhaps we agree to disagree while living together in a common Quaker "way." Many modern Quakers come to the Society of Friends having already had experience of other religious faiths and sects, so they bring with them a different inward knowledge and experience, formed over time. Sometimes they are reacting against a religion they have rejected. Someone raised in an extremely strict Christian sect, which had oppressed her in childhood, said that she found great freedom, quirkiness and joy in Quakerism as an adult.

We acknowledge styles of Quakerism from different parts of the world that have vastly different beliefs and worship in entirely different ways – something that has evolved because of missionary efforts in the past. Some views, passionately held, may be problematic for unprogrammed Friends, but we try to hold together all the same because it is important for us to be in dialogue and to work together rather than finding difference and forming even more factions. There is always common ground to be found. Quakerism tries to look outwards into the world and join with others in a spirit of open inquiry, recognizing that there are no certain answers, only more seeking and questioning.

The word "God" triggers different reactions in Quakers – there are many interpretations arising from personal experience – and these are shifting constantly, both in the individual and the group. We do not share agreement over our use of the word and what we think it means, and many feel that this is a healthy place to be. However, many agree that the idea of "God" remains a mystery, so we are at least united in the idea of not knowing and of seeking and experimenting.

In the adaptations of Fell's writings in this book, I have played with phrases such as "that of God" and "the spirit of God." Some Friends I have tried these phrases out on love experimentation with words and thoughts and find it helpful, but others do not, even finding it offensive. Therefore, the phrases are offered in the spirit of "not-knowing" and "trying to investigate," with the idea of broadening out the idea of "God," a word many find off-putting and veer away from. Some reject all religion because of it. "God" is only a word, but perhaps "that of God," originally coined by George Fox, one of the founders of Quakerism, though not intended to replace the word "God," helps to suggest qualities of God, whatever we feel these are and however we interpret the word. They are there for us to discover in the flow of life, within us and without, converging and moving inward and outward, in all things and in all places, in the spirit of connectedness. We all have "that of God" as a potential and in my imagination it is the Light that Fell talks about. I originally toyed with a different word: "Godness," but while some people I put it before warmed to it, others were horrified. I could see that if some were put off by it, then almost certainly others would be too. But then others, too, are put off by the word "God." It's possibly a waste of energy even trying to explore all the angles and getting caught up in what we think others are thinking and associating with certain words and phrases. But we can be united in "Something" and be "Something-ists," perhaps? And from that position of not knowing we can explore together. I have no doubt that Margaret Fell, if she could witness such ideas and views, would be shocked – but perhaps intrigued at the same time.

Personal beliefs and experiences

I wanted to look at some beliefs and experiences and explore where they came from. In this exercise, Fell's words were a jumping-off point. I aimed to return to first principles, the things that first brought Quakerism into being. In these I felt that I might reconnect with Quaker roots and find meaning; a reason why I had remained a member of the Society of Friends all my life, but without quite knowing why and without asking myself serious questions about it. I am pleased to have been born into Quakerism and never wanted to leave it or look elsewhere, but this has led to complacency and a sense of being in a comfort zone. I have found Quakerism to be deeply satisfying as well as challenging, part of my rootedness and my home on this planet. What could Fell have to say to us, speaking from the distance of the seventeenth century? What might be relevant for us today? What do we need for today?

Quaker "beliefs"

What do Quakers "believe"? This is an oft-asked question, which Quakers usually struggle to respond to, sometimes causing irritation and impatience. And there is no straight answer because we do not necessarily "believe" and if we do, it may not necessarily be belief in the same thing. How can we know? If we do hold beliefs, they come about through direct personal experience and cannot necessarily be framed and expressed in easily understood words – even for ourselves. However, there is perhaps an awareness among Friends that beliefs cannot be nailed down, that they change for the individual due to continuing inquiry – we are asked to be "open to new light from wherever it may come" in our *Advices and Queries* – and everyone is open to different forms of "new light."

If we are asked about Quaker beliefs, if we acknowledge that there are any, the first thing we have to do is ask the person what they are *really* asking about. For example, if they want to know what Quakers think about the word "God," we must ask the inquirer what they think "God" is before trying a response. Therefore, if we ask a group of Quakers the same question we may get a wide variety of answers, possibly after much hesitation. These may vary from the person who believes that God is a human construct, to the Christian Quaker who even perhaps refers to the Trinity, assuming that this forms part of Quakerism, which it does not. Many Quakers couch their words carefully and tell you what they do *not* believe, which can sound negative and too full of uncertainty to attract interest because many people seek certainty and do not necessarily want to do the searching, the hard work, themselves. This can be quickly followed by explanations about what we do *not* do in our Quaker practice, as opposed to what we *do* do. I have quite possibly been guilty of confusing a new attender and putting them off with what sounds like a message of negativity. But what do I believe? Or what have I discovered?

There have been many people and experiences, not to mention books and courses, which have influenced me along the way. But what have I learned experientially? Do I really think I have experienced the guiding hand of an external or internal force? Or is this just wishful thinking or part of my subconscious at work? Is "the mystery" just part of the human condition? Because I would love to think that there is a guiding hand of an external force. But have the things that have "occurred" *seem* to have happened because I have been in a receptive state and have wanted that to be the case? Or are they a part of external reality – nothing to do with me?

I recently met a group of Quakers from another part of the

worldwide Quaker diaspora, whose numbers are many times greater than ours in Britain. We were discussing number 42 from *Advices and Queries*:

> We do not own the world, and its riches are not ours to dispose of at will. Show a loving consideration for all creatures, and seek to maintain the beauty and variety of the world. Work to ensure that our increasing power over nature is used responsibly, with reverence for life. Rejoice in the splendour of God's continuing creation.

Different and the same

It quickly became clear that our belief systems and ways of worship differed vastly. Our conversations centered around the words "rejoice" and "creation," which pointed up differing ways of worship, beliefs, interpretations of what the word "God" means, what biblical teachings mean, and all the issues that flow from these things. Perhaps the thought that arrived with me was: "How can we both be called Quaker?" because it seemed hard to find common ground and there are other issues that we disagree vehemently on. However, what became clear was that although we are very different, we are still all Quakers who can talk to each other with kindness, patience, love, openness and a willingness to listen and learn, finding "that of God." And that seems to be the vital, central issue. Perhaps we are together "within" a state of difference. Perhaps what might start to unite all in the Way of Quakerism are the Testimonies: Simplicity, Truth, Equality and Peace (and variations of these words) and these form a loose structure by which we can all start individual explorations in Quakerism.

Finding our own way

Part of the attraction unprogrammed Quakerism, on a personal level, is that we have to battle our way through the undergrowth of ideas and experiences ourselves. And that gives us confidence to feel that what we find is real. No one is going to tell us what to believe – they are only going to try to encourage and draw us out. And that is a huge relief. The hard work involved in being engaged in a religious society that looks to the personal experience of the individual in worship for shape and form means that personal outcomes can be hard-won, though they are all the richer for it. If we haven't been given anything except a blank canvas, the picture we paint on it comes from within, bringing great personal reward and fulfillment. It reminds me of a little family firm I used to work for. The people were rooted in their mission and trusted the workforce to find ways of working that best suited them as individuals. They didn't really mind how we worked as long as the projects came in on schedule and on budget. So there was a high degree of flexibility, self-motivation and sense of responsibility. There was no rigid structure and the hierarchy was fairly flat. People weren't defined by their job descriptions. This suited me so well that I stayed there for many years – far longer than I was expecting to. I felt respected and valued and as a consequence learned much and carried out fulfilling, meaningful work. That is similar to my experience within the Society of Friends. I am expected to find my own way and I am trusted to do this in the way that suits me best, though within a solid framework. Help and guidance are available if necessary.

Out of this free-flowing approach I have come to my own conclusions about my "beliefs" (though perhaps "beliefs" are a sort of security blanket or comfort zone in which we can feel secure) – and they have changed dramatically over the years – from theism to atheism to panentheism and back to theism again, with a lot of uncertainty in between. No one has ever sat me down, not even as a child, and told me what to believe and this has freed me up to explore in my own way and arrive at whatever conclusions fit me best, but under the Quaker roof.

This has been an enormous privilege and a freedom, which I value highly. It has given me the right to answer searching questions about my beliefs with "it's a work in progress" and acknowledge that I might never reach a conclusion – though I am far more secure in my belief, or non-belief, than I once was. Is this a cop-out? I'd like to think not. I have a right to keep revising my views and, in Quakerism, am answerable to no one but myself and the "other." Marcus Borg talks about "beloving" rather than "believing," and this seems to be a far more helpful way of thinking. The great thing is to remain open, which is tough when part of being human seems to be to keep searching for what appears to be certain.

A new attender sat beside me in business meeting and asked me to explain what she could expect to take place. She had to ask whether she could come to the meeting and I felt bad that she had had to ask – we tend to assume that everyone knows that they can. Then I found myself explaining as much as I could about what might happen and why, and I became increasingly aware that what I was saying sounded if not unusual, perhaps even odd. We assume that, for example, "waiting in Spirit in order to make a decision as one body" is perfectly normal behavior because we are so used to it. But we forget that a newcomer might easily find it peculiar, or worse. But on the other hand they might find it wonderful. This occasion reminded me forcefully about how important it is to talk to each other, all the time, and to explain to people why we do what we do. This has the plus of allowing us to think and re-think things through and being able to articulate them, answering searching questions if necessary.

On a personal level, being a Quaker is more "process" than "system" and each one of us is responsible for our own progression, or otherwise – or even our own stagnation. We have a duty to ourselves to investigate and explore, without having boundaries imposed by others and without imposing them on ourselves. We start with our own experience in the stillness and silence of the meeting and allow the inward guide to take us further – or not. We must not worry if nothing seems to happen because we can start afresh every time we go. We are slightly different every time and life has changed us since last time. We are never the same people twice. We try to sit with openness and "not knowing," in order to explore and learn experientially. Holding on to a fixed belief might prevent us from finding out new things.

There are ideas to contemplate and absorb, contained in books such as *Quaker Faith and Practice,* a collection of extracts from the seventeenth century to the present day, updated each generation, and *Advices and Queries,* a small booklet which suggests how we might view life and live in faith. But mostly Quakerism can be distilled down to the physical practice of sitting with others in outward and inward stillness and waiting in Spirit, seeking and searching. As a group activity this becomes "corporate stillness," from where, perhaps, one is led to live out faith in action in the wider world. This religious practice is about self-exploration, but undertaken in a group, with no end to the process of exploring and of discovering. Perhaps you never actually arrive at a destination, but you can get glimpses of little arrivals.

However, you can also hit long periods of spiritual fallowness or wilderness, when nothing seems to be there and nothing seems to be happening. There is no creed to help you along, no fixed belief system in place to adopt or reject. Confusingly, there may seem to be many different things happening all at once. Some Friends are focused on Peace or Sustainability, some on Spirit in a general way, some on Christianity, some not. Many are concerned about action in the world, while others are holding Spirit quietly within. There is connection between all, even though approaches may seem disparate and unconnected. However, people follow their own passions and concerns and ultimately it really does feel as though everything is connected in Spirit.

In periods of confusion and feeling as though nothing is leading anywhere, all we can do is to keep on attending meeting for worship, being involved, talking to others, reading and absorbing fresh ideas and perhaps shifting forwards, inch by painful inch. Sometimes it might seem as if time might be running out. Other aspects of life get in the way and may be distracting. Panic may set in. Quakerism seems hard – and it is. But it is all the better for this. No one tells us what to think – they only offer a "tender hand" in a setting of trust and love, though sometimes this might feel like tough love. It is in the very difficulty of the struggle to discover that "the Life" can be experienced.

Reading Fell

When I started reading Fell's words they hit me forcefully. She spoke to me and I felt great emotion well up. In an instant I knew why I was a Quaker. Deep inside I said "Yes!" and punched the air. Doubts melted away. Her language is sometimes obscure and not what we might be comfortable with today. Her words sometimes seem judgmental. But I felt her passion and could connect with it. Overall meaning seemed to come through. I could identify with her and feel her power come alive. I could tell that she was unafraid to speak her mind and instruct others in what she felt they "should" believe. Her views are certain and confident – sometimes hard-hitting; definitely no-nonsense. Re-reading her writing about the moment she was "convinced" I felt the force of her certainty and her emotion. She spoke to me and every time I re-read that piece of text I reconnect with that convincement process and feel something of what she was going through. I found, as I read on, that ideas were repeated, as she was writing separately to different people or groups of people, adjusting for different audiences. Therefore her ideas come through again and again, perhaps in slightly different ways, and this started to have the effect of driving home certain images – Light being the central one, as part of Truth.

After a few weeks of transcribing Fell's words, I realized that she repeatedly tells us to "Turn to the Light" and "Stand in it," "Walk in it." Her message started to hit home and the phrases worked like mantras. But they were not as easy and soothing as I had first thought. They challenge us – and then challenge us again – to examine our own thoughts and actions and then do more, and then more again. They encourage us to go deeper. Some of the language is off-putting – far from comforting. It is a struggle to read and fathom her meaning. I wanted to bathe in, and be healed by, beautiful words, but this was not to be. There is a hard lesson here. Some of the writing is uncomfortable, even admonishing.

Fell's experience

Fell writes of George Fox's visit to her home Swarthmoor Hall, Ulverston, England, and how she went to her local church with him, hearing his words as he questioned the religious teachings and preachings of the day. She was hit by their power, in that moment, and this prompted great fundamental changes in her, which never left her and led her to her vital role in working to form the Society of Friends.

And [Fox] said "Then what had any to do with the Scriptures, but as they came to the Spirit that gave them forth. You will say, Christ saith this, and the apostles say this; but what canst thou say? Art thou a child of Light and hast walked in the Light, and what thou speakest is it inwardly from God?

This opened me [Fell] so that it cut me to the heart; and then I saw clearly we were all wrong. So I sat me down in my pew again and cried bitterly. And I cried in my spirit to the Lord, 'We are all thieves, we are all thieves, we have taken the Scriptures in words and know nothing of them in ourselves'… I saw it was the truth, and I could not deny it; and I did as the apostle saith, I 'received the truth in the love of it'. And it was opened to me so clear that I had never a tittle in my heart against it; but I desired the Lord that I might be kept in it, and then I desired no greater portion." Margaret Fell, 1694

Fell here has a moment of realization in which she knows inwardly that teachings from the church pulpit are secondhand information, not experienced directly by the congregation. She blames herself, feeling that the congregation, herself included, have "stolen" the words and made them their own but without really experiencing them firsthand. She realizes that what we must do is know them for ourselves in our souls; we must experience them personally and that we have the ability to do that. Fell had been seeking for some years before this convincement, and she risked much to become part of the embryonic Quaker movement. But from this starting point, Quakerism developed as a religious sect which expected to experience at firsthand and which had no need for intermediaries between the individual and divine source, therefore no clergy to interpret and present whatever they thought God's message might be. Each person, young and old, rich and poor, educated and uneducated, has the potential to experience God's word for themselves, within themselves. We are self-taught, experientially, and we have that power within us at all times and forever. We need look no further for our guide through life.

How to use Fell's writings

Excerpts from *A Brief Collection of Remarkable Passages …* by Margaret Fell, have been chosen for their mentions of the words "simplicity," "truth," "equality" and "peace." They are arranged in boxed-off sections and scattered throughout this book, offered, with modern adaptations and some personal ideas, for readers to use as they wish. They can be read aloud, meditated upon and then perhaps discussed in study groups.

Chapter 1

Simplicity

Try to live simply. A simple lifestyle freely chosen is a source of strength. Do not be persuaded into buying what you do not need or cannot afford. Do you keep yourself informed about the effects your style of living is having on the global economy and environment? *Advices and Queries*, number 41

* * *

Therefore as you tender your own Souls, and your Eternal Good, keep in the fear of the Lord, and be low, that the Plant of the Lord may take Root downward in you: And that none of you fly up above your Measure, and so the airy Spirit get into the Imagination, and there rest, and make an Image like Truth; and so you eat that which is forbidden, and break the Command of the Lord, and so betray the **Simplicity** and vail that which is Pure of God; which, if you are constant in Obedience to it, it will preserve in the **Simplicity**, and lead out of the Pollutions of the World, and the Filthiness of the Flesh; in that which is pure, you worship God in Spirit and in Truth: And now is the Lord seeking for such Worshippers in this his Day; which Day makes manifest, who turns out of the Eternal and Invisible, into the Imaginations, or Images or Forms, though it be of the Everlasting Truth; if it be only a Form, or a Colour, it cannot stand, but it is seen, and discover'd, and known where the Lord rules.
'An Epistle of M. Fell to Friends, 1654', from *A Brief Collection of Remarkable Passages* (p. 54)

Adaptation

"As you look inward and think about what might be good for you, respect God, be humble, so that the spirit of God can take root in you properly. And beware of going beyond your potential, letting your imagination run wild, and remaining in this exaggerated state for too long, so that your Truth is not real, so that you take ownership of things which aren't really yours and go against God, and so fly in the face of simplicity and conceal the purity of God. If you pay attention to God, it will keep your life in simplicity and lead you away from the baseness of the world and the wild ways of bodily temptations, so that all is pure and you come to God in Spirit and in Truth. God searches for such simplicity and comes alive in our minds in this way, rather than being portrayed in images and forms. If God is only a tangible form or even a color for us, it does not really have substance, even though we can see it right in front of us."

Ideas and notes

Here Fell seems to be highlighting the importance of simplicity of belief in terms of self-care of Spirit within. We all have a duty of care – for ourselves. In this we have to be humble and open to what might come to us, unbidden. If we are not open we block possibility and that of God cannot happen within us. We might be inclined to take on high-flown ideas that are the work of the ego, which are not Spirit-led, and these might prevent us from experiencing Truth and Purity as a reality. Fell also cautions against outward forms and our tendency to imbue something outside ourselves with Truth/purity/Spirit. She even says that color might be an outward form. Is this one of the places where plainness of dress in Quakerism originated? Perhaps Fell felt that Friends should concentrate on inner simplicity and simplicity of belief. For quite a significant time Friends wore only the plainest clothing in their search for simplicity before God and presumably as a demonstration of faith to the "world."

Now, Friends, deal plainly with yourselves, and let the Eternal Light search you, and try you, for the good of your Souls, for this will deal plainly with you, it will rip you up, and lay you open, and make all manifest which lodgeth in you, the secret Subtlety of the Enemy of your Souls, this Eternal Searcher and Tryer will make manifest.

from *A Brief Collection of Remarkable Passages* (p. 95)

Adaptation

"Friends, be honest with yourselves, and let the Light search within and look into your depths, for your own good, for the Light will deal honestly with you, it will open you up and reveal everything that is inside you, everything that might work against you, the Light, which searches and tests, will reveal."

Ideas and notes

Fell uses the word "plain" to describe the simple honesty of the Light in looking within and revealing all – bringing everything out into the open.

In a bare space, where there is little to distract us, we find the freedom to focus on what is really important and what is really there.

In a complex world, maintaining simplicity is more important than ever, but it can be a challenge. Perhaps its meaning and its importance lie in dispensing with all that is unnecessary and stripping away everything that is superfluous, so that we can experience continuing revelation of what really matters – the "other" or "that of God." Margaret Fell and the early Quakers certainly felt that this was a priority and were reacting against what they felt to be the falsehoods of the distracting physical "forms" found in churches.

There are many ways of expressing simplicity – outwardly and inwardly. Early Friends felt that removing and avoiding unnecessary outward detail and decoration would lead people more easily to God. Memories of Quakerism in the 1950s and 1960s reveal more emphasis on living "plainly" than seems evident today. As a child this seemed somewhat joyless, though perhaps some of the lived experience was as a result of post-war austerity and was the case for many people, not just Quakers. Color, artistic and cultural pursuits seemed frowned upon by many Friends; a legacy of earlier times when Quakers felt that such things distracted from the "true" pursuit of attending to God. Happily, that approach has largely died out as the Society gradually embraces broader ideas, for example, that all life, including creativity and artistic expression, is part of the state of being in God.

However, clutter, physical and mental, is possibly more of a distraction than it was a few decades ago. It now seems, in our age of excess, access to information and the feeling that there is always "more" threatens to dominate all aspects of our lives. Physical clutter can get in the way of mental clarity and Truth. Today we might be attracted to the idea of plainness, plain dress and plain living, but even these can become part of the complexity of life and the "things" of modern life continue to tempt us. Thinking about how to minimize purchases to what is really necessary, avoid waste and repair things rather than buying new, for example, can become complex obsessions in themselves, distracting from Simplicity. Quakers today seem far more a part of the world than formerly and are vulnerable to the same pressures and temptations as everyone else. "Retail therapy" may be experienced in the charity shop and it is still part of the same urge to acquire things. The richness of things, the color, texture, the plenty, accessibility, choice and the temptation to possess more and more is there to lure us and to test us.

The word "sustainability" has come to the fore in Quaker circles as well as the wider world. Our planet cannot support our ever-increasing demands and higher and higher consumption levels. It is starting to fight back and is ceasing to function healthily. How can we continue like this? A truly simple life might lead to a sustainable life, but we are now a long way down the road to planetary ruin. Where can we find hope?

The first time I visited Margaret Fell's home, Swarthmoor Hall, was a few days after a bereavement. I needed to sit with grief and reconnect with "other" in the flurry of shock, sadness, decisions and arrangements. It was a pilgrimage. At Swarthmoor we found great simplicity and great peace, great openness and great love. Dark paneling, uneven flagstones, simple furniture and a few ancient domestic possessions drew us in, warmed us and calmed us, connecting us to early Quakers. To be in that place, where they had lived and worked was right for that day: reminders of a simpler life was a balm and comfort. Tracing with our fingers the initials G. F., hammered into George Fox's trunk, enabled a visceral connection with the Quaker past.

Simplicity Themes

Simplicity in plainness

Outward forms reflect the inward state but they also contribute to it too. If we sit in a quiet, unadorned space wearing modest, plain clothes we are more likely to be able to focus inwardly on the life of Spirit than if we are distracted by the ornate, by color, shape and form.

Quaker meetinghouses are plainly made and unadorned. They are simple in style and materials are of good quality. Design is pleasing and everything is made to be serviceable and lasting. Meetinghouses have always been like this and new ones are built in the same way. Originally they were designed to be a reaction against what was thought overblown and "idolatrous" decoration in churches, expensive gold leaf, the outward forms and crosses, which in early Quakers' minds were misleading. Today we think carefully about simplicity of style and color in meetinghouses. We avoid hanging anything on the walls. The idea is that we are confronted with ourselves, the group and with "other."

Some people still dress plainly in Quaker circles today even though plain dress was abandoned in the mid-nineteenth century because it was felt better to be able to blend in with society rather than stand out as different. At the start of Quakerism, dressing plainly was just about removing excess frills and showy details. Later, plain dress developed into obsessive severity, which made Quakers look different from others in an eccentric way. When Margaret Fell witnessed the beginnings of uniformity of dress and restrictions in her final years she thought it a "silly poor gospel" and seemed to feel that it might not do what it was meant to do – free Quakers to live out the simple life and reflect an inward state. Perhaps she thought it would detract from more important underlying issues about what living simply really meant. It seems as though dressing plainly turned into an "outward form" – the very thing that first Friends were trying to remove themselves from.

Attending a Quaker wedding in the 1950s, I was terribly disappointed to see that the bride was wearing a brown tweed suit. A few decades later I experienced a move in the opposite direction when I witnessed Quaker brides wearing flouncy white meringue-style gowns in fashion at the time. Perhaps this was a reaction to the plainness of what had been practiced before and a break-out from simplicity in the moment of happiness in celebration. If Margaret Fell had witnessed these two extremes, she might have counseled "celebration but moderation" in our enjoyment of the day. She might also have wondered whether "celebration," such a fashionable concept today, might be getting in the way of the search for Truth in the relationship. Is the couple's relationship "right" when held in the Light and searched by it? Is the collective witness of the gathered meeting discerned in Truth?

The worship of things

Today we have a huge problem: our relationship with the material world. We love it, yet we are destroying ourselves and all life through the production of things: our purchase and ownership of them. We have lost some of life's meaning through our adoration of the physical. Rather than appreciate a few good things we have come to lust after more and more of them, putting quantity, newness and fashion above quality and durability. We are all guilty of this mentality creeping up on us. We waste and discard at the drop of a hat and things are cheaply made, of low quality. There is great inequality in ownership of things: some people have too much while others do not have nearly enough and this sets up envy in our increasingly unequal society.

In the increasing secularization of society, the worship of things has overtaken the worship of God. Quakerism may be following society's secular lead if it discards the idea of God in order to appear more palatable to a society that doesn't want it or seek it.

The simplicity of ideas

On the subject of faith, or religion, I am cluttered. There is no simplicity of thought – the mind flits randomly. It is overly stimulated by conflicting information, theories – theism or non-theism? It is like an attic stuffed full of possessions – some old and well-worn, which probably need to be cleared out; others more recently fallen out of use, but I can't quite bear to throw them away; some which might be useful one day and need to be kept carefully – others that I might need tomorrow or the day after. I read one book and am enthused by what the author says. I read another, which seems to say the exact opposite, and am enthused by that too. I need simplicity of ideas, but is that to try to narrow down too severely and limit exploration in a quest for certainty? The simple idea "God is love" seems overly simple, but what about evil?

How can we find simplicity in all the information, thoughts, suggestions, ideas, challenges embodied in Quakerism – far from simple! There is sometimes an experience of panicky confusion, wondering which route to take, what to focus on, which book to read, what to really take a long look at, what to ignore.

The simplicity of silence and stillness

Silence, and the deeper quality of stillness, is the basis of unprogrammed Quaker meetings, the foundations on which worship is built. This style of worship allows us to go within, waiting, so that we can then move outward into action, perhaps. Sometimes there seems to be a reluctance to disturb stillness by offering ministry (though it is true that sometimes people are disturbed by silence and want to fill it with words). Ministry might disrupt the growth of silence and stillness within. The critical self may feel that words fail to come from a deep enough place but are more "a thought has just occurred to me which might be of interest to others." Stillness, which grows in the silence, seems to be a space at the center of life, around which everything else swirls.

My path with silence and stillness goes back to meeting as a child; ministry was hard to understand, easy to ignore. I gazed out of the high windows of the meetinghouse at the trees outside and felt carried away into God's world, as it seemed in my interpretation. In that space of waiting, I found solace and creativity. My mind hung or hovered, creating a space for something to arrive. It was as though two silences, inner and outer, were converging, recognizing one another and finding harmony and meaning.

The old meetinghouse (built in 1820, bridging the eras of Quaker "quietism" and "evangelism") had a magical atmosphere, with its high, plain windows, rectangular arrangement of hard wooden benches, disused raised elders' pews looking out over the gathered Friends below and the separate women's meeting room outside with a screen between, which could be raised to form a single room. Elders, who also took the role of Overseers, once sat on such raised-up seats. Although anyone in meeting could minister, the seats were built so as to be physically above the rest of the meeting. Not so simple and not so equal.

The fabric of the building seemed to hold the stern but kindly ghosts of earlier Quakers and I imagined them sitting quietly there in their black hats and white bonnets – someone had possibly shown me a copy of the old painting of Christ amongst the worshipers in Jordans meetinghouse (*The Presence in the Midst* by James Doyle Penrose, 1862–1932). Looking at a postcard version of the painting now, the benches and their configuration with the raised Elders are exactly the same as the ones I knew.

Special children's literature, such as *The Book of Brave Quakers* by Elizabeth F. Howard, now seem laughably stiff and patronizing. We had little in the way of formal children's groups and so I was left to my own devices, to make what I wanted of it all. Perhaps this was a good way to introduce children to meeting – to let them find their own way in the silence; to have to face themselves in it. In the end, this is what we all have to do, on our own and in our own way. I recently saw a new illustration from *Let's Explore the Quaker Way*, showing Quakers, young and old, sitting in meeting. There is an atmosphere of glowing cosiness and bliss; rest and warmth. Each person holds an image of Light within themselves – even the child's toy rabbit does, as well as the bunch of flowers. Each version of the Light is different. It is a charming and appealing way of explaining some aspects of Quakerism to children (and to adults too).

Different kinds of silence

Since my childhood experience of Quakerism, I've found silence and stillness to be vital in many aspects of life. Silence allows Spirit to work. In other contexts, there are varying types of silence. For example, there is the silence of expectancy, when the conductor allows a preparatory pause between raising the baton and starting the piece of music, or a silence of completion, when a gap is allowed at the end of the performance, before the audience starts to applaud. This allowance for silence seems right – it gives space between one thing and the next, to let Spirit speak, to let "other" happen.

You can compare different types of silence and perhaps feel that Quaker silence in the meeting for worship is special and different. We tried out a series of drop-in silences for both Quakers and non-Quakers and sat in the same meeting room, in the same chairs, in the same circle. The silence was for rest and contemplation: no worship or "religion" as such. The resulting silence was substantially different from that of a meeting for worship. It was really just that: silence. Why was it so different? Perhaps in the gathered meeting there is an intention to focus on "other," both within and without.

Within the gathered silence of the meeting for worship are different kinds of silence. Far from being absence of sound, for there are always sounds, the particular silence in meeting can be different at the beginning, middle and end of the hour. The first few minutes of meeting may seem the most full and meaningful and the silence has a powerful "opening" quality, in which we are all settling and making ourselves available to whatever might happen. We are there in the moment. Later the silence seems to gather weight and become "heavy", like a vehicle gathering speed. It may be like wading through thick mud or groping through dense mist, though without getting stuck or lost. This is what the gathered meeting seems to be: when everyone's thoughts and focus seem settled, concentrated. We may all be contemplating different things, but we seem to have common focus. The silence seems charged and this is enhanced if there is physical stillness, with absence of coughing, shuffling or shifting. Everyone seems poised on the brink of a precipice and whether this then leads to jumping off into the precarious flight of vocal ministry and the chasm of not quite knowing where the words are leading, or not, is a question of personal leading. If something has occurred in the world, such as an accident or an attack, or if a member of the meeting has died, then you can feel the weight of common thought in the silence, which seems to be a vehicle for it. It is almost tangible. Perhaps you could even say that this is really all one thought. The silence seems full and made heavy with a single thought, which emanates from one point, or source. If we are all part of it and if it is part of us, having a common thought is not so outlandish. The silence is, perhaps, an organizing mechanism for joint thought. It seems, then, that some aspect of Quaker spiritual practice is concerned with silence being a vehicle for the connection of inner silence with outer silence and common connection with each other's inner silences. It is like a connecting thread.

Silence is something rather than nothing. It is not absence, but rather the thing itself. And this is a key aspect of Quakerism. If silence is "something" rather than "nothing," it may even be "everything," into which all ideas can flow. I remember someone ministering about how she sometimes came to meeting and dumped all the stuff from her life into the silence in the room. She was surrendering her life to the hour. She was saying, "Here is my life, here am I." The space in the middle of the circle of people is perhaps a physical representation of the silence of meeting. It is a space-time in which people can surrender all the issues of their lives, positive and negative, and start to heal themselves and each other, or they can just sort through their pile and make sense of it, saving some things, discarding others.

Oneness in silence

In meeting, when we can experience "oneness" and a sense of being there together in silence – deeply connected, the atmosphere shifts and thickens. It is the love of the one in the group, of the group, and the sense that we are there together in

Spirit. All thoughts seem to be one thought. Spirit moves among individuals with one purpose. We are gathered in, as one, under the same Spirit. It is as though we are all being held gently by the same tender hands. There may be common thought, as in "I was thinking about that too" or "That thought came to me just before you got up to speak." A strong memory of a gathered meeting was when I was not actually in the meeting room but sitting just outside it, as doorkeeper, waiting before letting in latecomers. Suddenly I could feel something different, something extra-ordinary connecting us all. The atmosphere was different, changed, charged.

The simplicity of God

"God": a simple word, highly charged, but perhaps not such a simple subject. The idea goes round and comes back. Is there an enduring presence above and beyond us? Or is God within and without – in all things? Are we God and is God us? Or is God a human construct, devised by us, to help us get through the difficult times we have here on earth? And if we start to find a way through the mess, then why do we so easily revert to the imprinted images of childhood? It is hard to leave these unhelpful images behind. The idea of the theistic God is now hard for many to accept and so many Quakers embrace the non-theistic model or perhaps the position of "not knowing" and acceptance of "a mystery." Such views seem understandable and real and perhaps are distracting us from more worthwhile pursuits such as improving the state of the world. We need to put words and differences in "belief" behind us in order to work together, in faith and hope, towards building something better. If Quakers can broadcast this position more effectively than we currently are, perhaps we can attract more to our way rather than dying out, defeated in a frustrated lack of expression and explanation.

The message "God is love" arrived with me, within and

without, and I knew I had to take notice of it. It is simple and understandable. It cuts to the chase. And the experience of it could not be denied because it was a reality. This came after many years "in the wilderness," of not knowing, or only partially knowing, and constantly being uncertain. It came as a certainty – a "knowing."

Margaret Fell would almost certainly be mystified by any doubts we might have about belief in God. In her time the existence of God was a certainty and not questioned; it was accepted by all. She was secure in her faith and it was far from being a distracting series of concepts, to be constantly picked over. She might even accuse us of wasting precious time in our wondering, that we might better use our time doing good in the world.

Chapter 2

Truth

Are you honest and truthful in all you say and do? Do you maintain strict integrity in business transactions and in your dealings with individuals and organisations? Do you use money and information entrusted to you with discretion and responsibility? Taking oaths implies a double standard of truth; in choosing to affirm instead, be aware of the claim to integrity that you are making.

If pressure is brought upon you to lower your standard of integrity, are you prepared to resist it? Our responsibilities to God and our neighbour may involve us in taking unpopular stands. Do not let the desire to be sociable, or the fear of seeming peculiar, determine your decisions.
Advices and Queries, numbers 37 and 38

God is Light, and in him is no Darkness at all; the Word is Light, which shines in thy heart, if thou turn thy mind to this Light within thou wilt see from whence ariseth envy and strife, and all that is evil, that proceeds out of the heart; and now the Spirit being put in the inward parts, and the Law of God written in the heart, and the mind kept to this Light, this cleanseth, purgeth and washes the inward parts (viz. from Sin and Pollution) for who walk in the Light, the Blood of Jesus Christ cleanseth them from all Sin, and therein the Saints have fellowship one with another in the Light, and they who love the Light, it is their Teacher.
'Letter to the Queen of Bohemia', from *A Brief Collection of Remarkable Passages* (p. 34–35)

Adaptation

"That of God is Light, which has no darkness in its essence; the Word is Light and this shines in your heart. If you turn your attention to the Light inside you, you will see the source of all negative things. So now Spirit is inside you, you have God inside you too. If you stay focused on this, you will find that Light can cleanse you inwardly of the negative things, so that there is a place where we can all greet each other in its glow. Everyone who loves the Light can learn from it."

Ideas and notes

Fell writes that "God is Light" but that it contains no darkness. The darkness is all within us and we should employ the Light to identify our inner darknesses. So it is within our remit to look hard at the darkness and recognize it – to see what is being concealed there. Are we using the darkness to hide things, even from ourselves? We all have Spirit within us – so we all have the potential to use the Light to reveal our darkness and then do something about it. The Light is like a cleansing brush that can sweep out the dust and rubble inside us all, or a searchlight looking into all the dark places and revealing things as they really are. In this inner cleansed state we can all be together in recognition of the Light. For Quakers, this is important because we have no one to lead us, except ourselves, and we are equal, having only differences in experience, so we have to do the inner work and meet each other in Spirit in order to get things done and make sure things run smoothly. As a group we have to take responsibility and make difficult decisions sometimes, and so we have to meet in a place where Spirit can unite us and move us forward into action, so that we have the confidence to know that we are being led correctly in the right outcomes.

The Truth is one and the same always, and though ages and generations pass away, and one generation goes and another comes, yet the word and power and spirit of the living God endures for ever, and is the same and never changes.

Margaret Fell

Truth is the very core of that of God and of life. Truth is Truth. It is the "isness" that is and all that is. It is good to keep looking at what faith, belief and religion is, what purpose these things serve and how can we square them with our knowledge of the world today. What is the Truth of life and what is it for? Is religion a wonderful tool to help us find Truth, to flourish and find meaning in life, or is it a human construct, evolved by us to help make us feel safe, but which, in reality, can mean everything or nothing at all – something we have devised to answer our deepest questions? Is it "something" or "nothing"? Is it full or empty? Charged with meaning or a hollow sham? Are we spiritual beings trying to make sense of everything, searching for explanation as to what life is and why things happen, which just can't be explained, or are these things just a figment of the imagination – part of our desire for life to mean something when it just *is*? Are we grasping after something that really does exist or something that we need in order to satisfy our need for meaning? Is what we are seeking so complex that it's hard to take in, digest and hold on to or so very simple that we are missing it in all the complexity that we create for ourselves? Hidden in plain sight.

Today "Truth" is talked about as being something that is far from fixed and certain. We are said to be living in a "post-truth world," where we have to find what is true through trial and error. We do not know whether to accept what we are told via the media or whether we are being sold falsehood, as part of someone else's agenda – particularly in the world of politics. This makes us untrusting and suspicious. We become unconfident about using the tools of technology, which our clever brains have devised for our convenience and efficiency. How do we know that everything is what it seems to be? How can we avoid falling victim to those who peddle untruths? The dark side of human ingenuity has always found ways of playing around with Truth.

In Fell's time, Truth was Truth, without doubts and uncertainties. Personal integrity was perhaps more highly valued then and Quakers were well known for their trustworthiness and straight-dealing in all matters, business and otherwise. In a society that bought and sold using a bargaining system, every purchase was haggled over, so that some people were paying more than others and the gullible were being swindled, Quakers pioneered the fixed-price system. Today it seems common practice to tell small lies and embroider truth to save face or even to protect another's feelings, not to mention carry out fraud, so perhaps Truth is valued less now than it was.

Truth Themes

Christianity lies at the heart of Quakerism, but what Truth does this have for us today? Is Christianity about living out the teachings of Jesus in our lives?

The truth of the cross

I have always noticed the cross and have been drawn to it as an image, despite feeling that it is not "Quakerly," whatever that means, and I have felt a sense of guilt about noticing it at all, let alone dwelling on it. But the image seems to have Truth at its core. I could not and cannot ignore the cross. I started to see the image in the chance juxtaposition of a horizontal line with a vertical one – in buildings, nature and small found objects. And I started to seek these images out in photography. I was mysteriously drawn to the shape. What does the cross really mean? I could not ignore its power.

At Easter, I came across a real man on a real cross in a local open space. He resembled our usual Western version of Christ, down to the long bedraggled hair, the loincloth, the punishing crown of thorns and the specks of "blood." I felt something shift within me. The tableau, complete with Roman centurions brandishing leather whips, turned out to be a local group of actors advertising an Easter Passion, but the effect was dramatic and realistic. I felt repelled and attracted simultaneously. Perhaps Christian roots are more strongly imprinted than I had thought.

An image that has remained in my mind is of Diane Arbus's photograph of the woman sword-swallower. Head thrown back and arms stretched on either side, the woman is consuming the sword, the hilt creating a cross and her arms and body forming another. A cross within a cross. On one level this is everywoman "becoming the cross" in revealed strength.

I sewed some "soft" crosses. These seemed to satisfy my need for the strength of the symbol of two intersecting lines. Their texture and color appealed to my need for beauty and creativity. I wanted to adjust the harsh message and make it approachable. The crosses were like soft toys – stuffed fabric and embroidery with beading. The colors were vibrant and joyous. Some were small enough to clench in the hand and squeeze and this felt comforting. Some people recoiled from them while others found them amusing and cuddly. Making them helped me integrate the image.

Living under the cross

To live in the power of the cross or "under" it seems to mean that the Christ within governs our whole being and that we live life with Christianity and its teachings at the front and back of our minds at all times; it informs each and every aspect of life. Early Quakers took the cross to be an inner crucifixion: what Christ had gone through in the body was now taking place within the soul and resurrection was to be a continuing process for all.

Light as Truth

Early Quakers took the idea of "Light" from the first chapter of the Gospel of John.

> In the beginning was the Word, and the Word was with God, and the Word was God.
>
> The same was in the beginning with God.
>
> All things were made by him; and without him was not any thing made that was made.
>
> In him was life; and the life was the light of men.
>
> And the light shineth in darkness; and the darkness comprehended it not.
>
> There was a man sent from God, whose name was John.
>
> The same came for a witness, to bear witness of the Light, that all men through him might believe.
>
> He was not that Light, but was sent to bear witness of that Light.
>
> That was the true Light, which lighteth every man that cometh into the world.
>
> *John 1, 1–9*

The word "Light" – used by early Quakers to convey all that is mysterious or ineffable – reveals Truth and it can reveal our Truth, today, now. Light is the way Truth can be made real. It is a metaphor for "God" or "energy" and many other ideas, such as "seed," "Father and Mother" or "whatever you want to call it." We all have Light. "Light," whether we experience this is an inward Light flowing to the center from an outside source, or an "inner" Light that already lies within, or even, perhaps, a flow moving in both directions and connecting all as a single entity. Light is there inside us all; an interior guide. It is up to each one of us to pay attention to it or ignore it, then whether we do something or do nothing, are busy or remain still, whether we do good or do harm, whether we love or hate. We listen to what the Light is telling us and the stillness of a meeting for worship, with others, is the place where this might happen. Margaret Fell, in many places in her writings, asks us to look within to see what the Light can reveal to us about Truth, our own Truth, whether "good" or "bad." As Quakers, without the concept of original sin, we are nonetheless asked to see what is really there and then what we can do about it, as far as we are able. What can Light reveal?

A vision of Light

As a child, the symbol of Light was important to me. It was something I could see and understand and I quickly associated it with the quality of God. I had a vision of an outward God, as it seemed to me then, bathing me in a special pool of light, like a spotlight. This seemed to be light coming from an outside source.

A word that matters

"Light" seems to embody Truth. It is the word that Fell, Fox and others first used to describe the power of Spirit within all, which can be called God or perhaps comes "from God." It is a useful word when trying to articulate that of Spirit. You can use it to describe an idea or an inspiration, a calling or the inner voice. And you can use it to talk about the dark corners of the self, which can be exposed or explored by using that Light. We can become "enlightened" by the Light. Or we can "throw Light on" something to let it become clearer. We can "hold someone in the Light" if we want to pray for them and there is a common understanding of what this means.

Turrell's "Skyspace"

An installation made by Quaker artist James Turrell is striking because of what he has to express about Light and, by extension, Truth. From the outside, the Skyspace looks like a grassy hummock. You approach down a pathway and enter a narrow tunnel. You are directed into a circular chamber with a bench seat around the perimeter. It is very similar to the small circular meeting room in the Quaker Centre in Friends' House, London. Inside the Skyspace your gaze is drawn upward. Being there feels very much like worship. There is a large hole in the ceiling, open to the sky – blue with passing clouds – it changes with the weather. This hole is like a circular frame, focusing on the patch of sky in view. It is different from looking up at the sky when there is no frame. It is a concentrated view. The clear blue is accentuated by the pale ceiling. The hard sunlight hits the wall and makes dynamic shadows. The effect is starkly simple. Below, set into the floor, is a circle of blue stone – like a reflection or a pool of water in a forest. You feel encouraged to see what light is and what it can do. You marvel at it. You are acutely aware of the presence of Light. The installation can never be the same twice because light is constantly changing. Turrell talks about how we are co-creators of our own reality – so his work is there to be seen, but it is up to us to add our own selves to the experience of seeing it. We are in, and of, the Light.

Fell and Light

Fell writes a lot about Light and she had experienced its force in the clarity of her own convincement. In *A Brief Collection of Remarkable Passages* it seems that she gradually warms to her theme and comes at the subject from all possible angles, going ever deeper and extracting more and more meaning from the word. The Light shines in Christ and reveals the darkness of the soul, which is within all of us. We only have to have awareness of the Light for it to do its work and revelation. Her ideas originate in fall-redemption theology, so she talks about "sin" and "pollution" of the soul. Though I have often tried to reject this theology because it seems to get in the way of Truth and Light and moving forward in positivity, I can see the sense in having it as a construct and making the effort to work on it within. Fell's is as good a way as any, even though some of her words seem harsh and punishing. She poses a very tough challenge to us to be in the Light so that it can expose our dark sides. I give thanks to her for her unstinting courage, her tough words of challenge, her endurance and resilience. I think of her raising a large family and running an estate, much of the time single-handed, not to mention her incarcerations in prison and long, hard journeys around the country. Her convincement is impressive and makes us sit up and take notice. She showed great bravery in difficult times, in her willingness to face up to harsh difficulties and her unswerving pursuit of the Truth. Fell tells us to "stand in the Light" and see whatever darknesses it reveals. Her passionate words shake us awake and help us focus and see where we might be able to do more. In fact, she says that we MUST do this – or ... She is a tough and valuable guide.

If ye turn to the light which is my witnesse, and if ye hate the light, and turn from the light, the light is your condemnation. Margaret Fell, *A Brief Collection of Remarkable Passages etc, 1710*

The following Epistles were written at the first Appearance of **Truth** among us, when we were young in it: And the Light of Christ being our first Principle, our Minds being turned to it, and we believing in it, and it being become our Teacher, Leader, and Guider, we saw perfectly, that there was no Safety, nor Preservation of us out of Sin and Transgression, but as we obey'd the Light, and follow'd it in our Hearts and Consciences, and its leading out of Sin, Transgression, and Iniquity: And so as we waited in it, and dwelt in it, we came to witness a Washing and Cleansing by the blood of Jesus. 'Epistles of M.F's To Friends, &c.', *A Brief Collection of Remarkable Passages* (p. 45–46)

Adaptation

"The following epistles were written when Truth first appeared to us, when we knew little about it. The Light of Christ was a first principle for us, and we were already focused on it, believing in it. So it gradually became something that taught us things, led us and guided us. We realized that there was no way it could save us from sinning and transgressing, but that if we looked to the Light and followed its advice it might lead us away from all the negative things of life. So we did this by waiting in the Light and contemplating it and eventually we experienced ourselves being cleansed by Christ's Light."

Ideas and notes

Here Fell is writing to scattered early Friends and trying to offer encouragement and support. She relates how she and others gradually became aware that accessing Truth was not just bathing in the warm glow of the Light of Christ but waiting in stillness for its teachings, Truth might reveal the less wonderful things too, by shining revealing Light inwards, and be helpful in steering away from them. This realization, which needed no teaching except inner teaching, gradually turned into the Quaker practice of waiting in silence and stillness for clarity (Truth) to arrive, both to the individual and to the group. Fell states very clearly that this Truth cannot and will not prevent the person from thinking bad things or behaving less than perfectly, but that it can eventually lead the person away from them over time.

And so we came to discern betwixt the Precious and the Vile, and betwixt the Holy and the Unclean, and betwixt the Chaff and the Wheat; and between those that served God, and those that served him not. And when we came to this Sight, and Knowledge, and Discerning, then we became very Zealous for God, and for his **Truth**, and for the Preservation of his People in the **Truth**: And our Hearts became tender, and we had a pity for all People's Souls, that remained in the Darkness. And we were moved of the Lord to write often to Friends, and our Testimony was very much to the Light of Christ in the Conscience; because we saw that, That was the Way, and there was no other: For Christ Jesus said I am the Light; He also said, I am Way, the **Truth** and the Life; and there is none that can come to the Father, but by me.

A Brief Collection of Remarkable Passages (p. 46)

Adaptation

"So we eventually were able to tell the difference between what was good and what was bad, and what was of God and what was not, between chaff and wheat, and between those who followed God and those who did not. When we woke up to this knowledge and way of identifying the Truth, we became very protective of it and wanted to preserve it. We found ourselves empathetic with others and we felt we had to communicate with Friends, emphasizing our findings about the Light of Christ within, believing that this way was the way forward. We remembered Christ saying that he was the Light and the Way, the Truth and the Life and that this was the route to the spirit."

Ideas and notes

This piece concentrates on the idea of discernment of the Truth, how to distinguish between truth and untruth. Discernment is an important Quaker tool that underpins all our decision-making, individually and as a group. Fell is saying here that the Light searching within helped the group decide what was good and what was bad. What had to be retained and what had to be cast out. In practicing this process, the group grew to have more empathy for all. Having the confidence of the Light behind them, they could then help others. Something that might not sit so well with modern Quakers is the idea that Christ is the only route to that of God. Where does that leave all those who are not Christians?

> And also there being such a Body of Darkness, which warred against it; for People having lived in the Darkness, out of the Knowledge of the Light; it was such a new Doctrine to them, that there was a mighty War in People's Minds against it: And the Priests and Professors setting themselves against it, calling it a Natural Light; and some said, It was a dim Light; and some scoffingly call'd it, a dark Lanthorn; others said, It was not sufficient to condemn, So, in their dark Imaginations, they fought against it: And very much we had to do, in the beginning, to get People convinced of the **Truth**, and of the Sufficiency of it; and also, those that were convinced, to keep them in Obedience to it. But the Lord's Arm and Power carry'd on his own Work, notwithstanding all the Opposition of the Power of Darkness, Glory and Praises be to his Holy Name for ever.
>
> from *A Brief Collection of Remarkable Passages* (p. 47)

Adaptation

"There was, amongst people in general at that time, a groundswell of 'darkness,' which resisted the call to Light. People had lived in darkness for a long time and had no experience of the Light, so people turned away from this new idea. It was foreign to them and so they didn't like it. Also priests and those who thought they knew more than others were against it, calling it 'natural' light. Some said it was a dim light, others scoffed at the idea and called it a 'dark lantern.' Others said there wasn't enough evidence for it, and so naturally resisted the idea. So we had our work cut out for us to get people to be convinced of the Truth and the power of it. It was also a challenge for those who were already convinced to stick at it. However, the power of God persevered and opposed the power of darkness and so we offer praise forever."

Ideas and notes

This seems to be concerned with the natural human tendency to be skeptical and conservative. The word "darkness" seems to imply "uneducated" or "unenlightened." Many people hate change and new things. We see the same today when some people avoid modern technology and pine for the old ways, which are familiar and make us feel safe. Nostalgia rules. We also hear about the human need to "prove" everything, and this is particularly true today. People need scientific evidence to know that something is true and they can't just take something on trust.

So this God, who is a spirit, is unknown to all outward Worships, and to all Professions that are outward, to all you Athenians that are outward, and to all you Churches and Forms that are outward, though they be never so like the **Truth**, yet if you be not guided by the Light, and dwell in the Light, and taught with the Light, by which the Lord God teacheth his People, you shall never know the living God; but you hold the **Truth** in Unrighteousness, so long as your Minds are not guided by the pure Light in your Consciences, and the Righteous Law of God, which he writes in your Hearts, Christ Jesus is the end of the Law for Righteousness, and his Sceptre, is a Sceptre of Righteousness, and where he Rules, he Rules in Righteousness, and that which is of God, is a Witness of Righteousness …

from *A Brief Collection of Remarkable Passages* (p. 498)

Adaptation

"So that of God, or Spirit, is not experienced in worship or by that experience that faces outward into the world. These things seem to show Truth, but if you are not guided by Light and live in it, are taught by it, guided by it, learning from it – for this is how that of God works in us – you can never know of it inwardly.

Your Truth is instead held in that which is false. Because you are not being guided by the Light that shines within you already. Therefore, search within, so that you can be guided by the Light that lies inside all of us."

Ideas and notes

Fell is stressing that the Light, or that of God, is already working within us and does not manifest through looking outside ourselves. She asks us to be guided by the Light completely and live within it, using our experience as a tool.

Truth through discernment

The Truth seems to be a shifting thing today. People say whatever suits them best in the moment. Friends have always felt that it is important to be straight and honest all the time, to act with the utmost integrity in all things, in all areas of life. But how do we know what is Truth and what is not? How can we decide?

The discernment process has been used since the early days of Quakerism as a way of discovering God's will and deciding whether this is *really* what it is, or whether will is interfering. Discernment involves emptying the self and allowing the spirit to work without the mind intruding and a discerned outcome comes about through worship and searching in Spirit and letting the inward teacher guide and inform.

As individuals the discernment process is hard to use, though the "Experiment with Light" exercise, practiced by many Quakers today, can be very effective on a personal level. The Light is, perhaps, the place where Spirit and self come together and it can expose the positive as well as the negative. So Light can come from a different place, providing surprises, some not so welcome. But we have the gut feeling that it is coming from a place of Truth, that this is the Truth working within and trying to communicate.

However, it is hard for each of us to know whether an idea

or a solution is really the will of Spirit or whether ego and the brain are getting in the way by "thinking things through." As a group activity, however, Quaker discernment has a far greater chance of being successful because the individual must lay aside ego and focus on the good of the group. There is more openness to otherness.

Truth in creativity

How does a blank page become a printed book? How does the blank canvas become a painting hanging on a wall? How does a leading or a nudge become an action? How does nothing become something? How does a jumble of half-formed ideas suddenly take on significance and give us the awareness and confidence to go on to create something meaningful? Truth is at work here and it is a question of letting go of the ego, the doubting part of the self, the lack of confidence and seizing hold of Truth, in its essence. Truth takes over and guides us towards finding meaning in action. Suddenly things start to make sense and the activity becomes so important that it cannot be discarded. It must be followed through to the very end. In between bursts of practical activity and results, the mind and the subconscious carry on working, guided by Truth. Creative activity, when it happens, seems spontaneous, almost automatic, to be coming from a different place. There seems to be no effort involved. When further inspiration is needed, it seems to arrive without a struggle. Ideas flow and we are *in* that flow. We *are* that flow. Results have meaning and even the tiniest detail is charged with a rightness that brings everything together, in all aspects, as a cohesive whole.

Chapter 3

Equality

How can we make the meeting a community in which each person is accepted and nurtured, and strangers are welcome? Seek to know one another in the things which are eternal, bear the burden of each other's failings and pray for one another. As we enter with tender sympathy into the joys and sorrows of each other's lives, ready to give help and to receive it, our meeting can be a channel for God's love and forgiveness.

Respect the wide diversity among us in our lives and relationships. Refrain from making prejudiced judgments about the life journeys of others. Do you foster the spirit of mutual understanding and forgiveness which our discipleship asks of us? Remember that each one of us is unique, precious, a child of God.
Advices and Queries, numbers 18 and 22

Now, that every particular Member of the Body may be sensible of the Hardship and Suffering of others, and be willing and serviceable in their places, in what the Lord requires, and to remember that those that are in Bonds, as bound with them, and them that suffer Adversity, as you being your selves also in the Body, and that you may bear one another's Burthens, and be **equally** yoked in the Suffering.
from *A Brief Collection of Remarkable Passages* (p. 58)

Adaptation
"Now that everyone who is a part of the whole is aware of the suffering of others and is willing to assist them in what God requires, remember that we are all bound together in our joint

suffering, we can help each other in our sufferings and be joined equally in it."

Ideas and notes

"Equal" is used here to reinforce the idea that we are all members of one whole and we are all equally involved in the suffering of the group and joined together in it. There is something here about bearing the same responsibility as each other, which is hard, since in all groups a pecking order develops of those who seem more experienced than others and those who put themselves forward as leaders and those who hang back, wanting to merge into the background and follow. Despite the lack of hierarchy in modern Quakerism, or at least the existence of a fairly "flat" structure, there are always those who seem to take the lead, who are deemed more "weighty" than others. They do not necessarily mean to be like this; others may foist the label upon them. But it may make some of those others feel "lesser" and prevent those with less experience from coming forward and taking responsibility and roles. It stops some people feeling confident and able to nurture others as they might be willing to. Perhaps if there was a more forgiving atmosphere around tasks and responsibilities then people would feel less judged. As things stand, those with less experience often feel "less than" and worry about getting things wrong, making mistakes.

* * *

To feel that all are equal in that of God is paying homage to the quality of God in each other and in all creation too. It is to recognize the sacred in ourselves, in each other and to offer respect for that. The process of convincement, in which a Friend recognizes that God is already within and is not mediated by another is a recognition of the equal spiritual status of all.

Quakers have a testimony to equality; we all have the same,

equal, potential to find that of God. We are a priesthood of all believers, so feel that it is impossible for anyone to know more or be better than anyone else, except perhaps in the sense of acquired and learned knowledge.

In her writings, Fell is using the word "equal" or "equally" to mean either "the same as" or "to be right" – as in "correct." As used in her writings, the word appears to have small beginnings, as in being "just" and seems very close to Truth, but in the intervening centuries it has taken on a far greater meaning for Quakers. Our testament to equality is central to us in our thinking as a group and fundamental to our behavior within it.

Equality Themes

Equality in Quakerland

In a piece of Britain Yearly Meeting 2019 ministry we heard about attenders who did not join the Society of Friends because they did not feel "good" enough, and this has been heard from the most surprising people; people who are not only "good," if not "better" in their very cores, and who also have a lot to give others. This is surely not how we should view ourselves – as some being "better" than others.

How we project ourselves

This poses awkward questions about how people who are already members are projecting themselves as "members" and how they are, in turn, seen by attenders and inquirers. How might we be subconsciously excluding others? By behaving as being entitled, privileged, confident? Or by being modest and low-key – blending in to the background so that we are not seen too much and do not express important things about Quakerism. These are undesirable qualities and I wonder how we have unwittingly painted ourselves into this unequal, off-putting corner – crowded with mainly white, middle-class people of a certain age. Someone even commented that we form a group that is visually recognizable by styles of dress and personal choices – sometimes an unappealing image of "not caring about appearance." We laugh at ourselves, but shouldn't we be worried about the way we appear to others? We have developed a Society that is more or less reflecting one part of society only – a highly privileged one. We think we are being "equal" and inclusive, but are we not gathering together in a self-selected group of those who are very similar? We may not mean to be like this, but we are. By being seen in this way we are surely discouraging those who might want to join us – Quakerism is for all who want it and all who might benefit from it, so that they might benefit others too. We are all imperfect humans who are seeking. We surely have to work harder at seeing ourselves as others see us. But how could we then make changes that might eventually mean we were inauthentic, not "ourselves"?

Love – and more love

Perhaps the way forward is to express outwardly, demonstrably, more love, care, concern, and more warm welcoming and more fond care-giving to all – and then more love again. And we all have love to spare. Someone came to meeting who said that she was open to receiving some grandparenting – she had no grandparents of her own. Before she said this I had been worried that there were only a few younger people in the meeting for her to get to know. We have to be careful in our assumptions.

* * *

And again, the Lord saith unto Moses, how long will this People provoke me? And how long will it be ere they believe me, for all the Signs that I have shewed amongst them. So here you stand yet in the Unbelief and Hardness of Heart, and Stiff-neckedness, and now it is time for you to return unto the Lord, who calls you, and to believe on him, and hearken to his Voice within you, which testifies against all Sin, and all Unrighteousness, and all Unbelief, and Hard-heartedness, and Uncleanness, and this testifies against all Oppression and Wrong, there is that in your Hearts which tells you, that you should do unto all Men, as ye would they should do unto you. This is Just, this is Righteous, this is **Equal**. There is that in you which testifies against Lying and false Swearing, and bearing false Witness against your Neighbour. There is that in your Conferences which tells you, you should have no other God, but the living God, and that ye should not make any graven Image.

Now if you do not mind that of God in you, to guide you and lead you, you serve not the living God, but make an image in your Minds of him, which the Light of God in you lets you see is not the Truth.

from *A Brief Collection of Remarkable Passages* (p. 177)

Adaptation

"Again, the Lord said to Moses, how long will these people provoke me? And how long will it be before they believe me, for I have given them so many signs. So here you are standing amongst those who do not believe and those with hard hearts, and who are stubborn in their thinking, holding onto old ideas. Now it is time for you to return to God, which is calling you, and to believe in this, and listen to the voice inside you, which testifies against all sinning, everything that is not righteous, all lack of belief, and hard of heart, and all that is not clean, and this testifies against Oppression and Wrong, that in your heart tells you that you should only do to others what you would do to yourself. This is just, right and equal. There is that in you which testifies against lying and false oaths, and bearing false witness against others. There is that within you which tells you that you should have no other God but the one that lives within you, and that you should not make any images. So if you do not nurture God within you, to guide you and lead you, but instead make an image in your mind of this quality, the light of Truth inside you will tell you that this is not the Truth."

Ideas and notes

This piece is Fell speaking through God's words to Moses and, by extension, us. We are exhorted to go inside and hear the voice within, searching for all that is right and "equal." So the use of "equal" here is very much to do with rightness and justness – it is a "given" or "rule of law," "common sense." Each one of us has a strong sense of right and wrong and this is our moral compass, which we should use. That of God within all is a tool for our use – as a guide and leader and there is no place for the workings of imagination and the conjuring up of images, which may well be far from the Truth.

The Witness of God is just and **equal**, and can admit of no unclean nor defiled thing, but the pure Eternal Witness of the pure God presents every Man perfect in Christ Jesus. And so as you dwell and abide in the Light, ye that were sometimes Darkness, will be Light in the Lord, and ye that were afar off, will be made nigh by the Blood, as you dwell in the Light, and walk in the Light, where the Blood cleanseth and washeth from all Sin: For the Apostle saith, That God hath made all Nations of one Blood and Mold that dwell upon the Face of the Earth, and hath determined the Times before appointed, and the Bounds of their Habitation, that they should seek the Lord, if happily they might feel after him, tho' he be not far from every one of us.

from *A Brief Collection of Remarkable Passages* (p. 498)

Adaptation

"That of God always acts with justness and even-handedness,

and allows nothing that is less than perfect and good. That of God and its witness sees all people as perfect beings in Christ. As you rest in the Light, even if you were sometimes part of the Darkness, you will be viewed as being part of the Light of that of God, and if you felt a long way away from this state, you will be brought nearer to that of God as you stay in the Light and walk in it, being cleansed and washed of things that are bad: For the Apostle says, that of God made us all the same, whoever we are and wherever we are, so that we can come to that of God, if they are searching for this state, even if it is not far removed from where we are."

Ideas and notes

The spirit of God is the same for everyone and is fair in all things, whatever the circumstances. Whoever needs the Light can access it and live in it, no matter how far from it they are. Negative things will melt away.

The equality of women

The spiritual equality of women was one of the key elements of early Quakerism – women might have had different roles from men in life, but in Spirit they were equal. They were considered to be "the same" but with different purposes in the world. Their equality was greater in the early years of Quakerism than later on, it seems, when women's meetings were formed and they took on the more pastoral roles in the Society of Friends, perhaps losing something important. However, this may be a modern take on the equality of roles and the balance of the sexes. In our eyes it might feel "lesser" to be concerned with pastoral roles than with "important" decision-making, but to early Friends there was a more "different but equal" approach and everyone was assigned their place in the world according to their "measure" or ability, or potential.

All-age equality

In a truly equal society a child can have as much spiritual insight as an eighty-year-old and can be just as much a teacher or prophet to others. We acknowledge that anyone, young or old, can have the gift of prophecy and be able to put this into action. Equality means that it is up to each individual to be responsible for their own learning and insight. There are no levels of attainment, no beginnings and no ends and no hard and fast theology – except perhaps for the discoveries of early Friends, which form the basis of this book. There is just the Self in the stillness. It is experiential: when Spirit within moves us to act, whether to minister vocally in meeting for worship, to take up a particular Quaker role or to pursue a personal concern.

Women's speaking justified

Fell's most well-known piece of writing (*Women's Speaking Justified*) sets out the importance of the spiritual equality between the sexes, which Quakers initially upheld in the freedom for women to minister in meeting equally with men, even though she and George Fox, plus other early Quaker innovators, developed the system of separate men's and women's meetings. She asks that all people should be treated as having equal spiritual worth and potential under God; women being just as capable of ministering to others as men. Many women became well-known Quaker ministers, traveling in the ministry too. Although Quaker women have always been acknowledged as being equal to men spiritually, today they are still recovering from the division of roles that came about several centuries ago and we must remember our essential equal sharing with men and equality in all aspects of life.

We must always remember that God is Light, speaking through women just as certainly and clearly as through men. The certainty expressed throughout Fell's writings bears out her strong feelings about the equality of living in Light and the confidence of expression for all. Perhaps if Fell could see what goes on today, she would be surprised at the need for the Suffragette movement, then the rise of the Women's Liberation movement in the 1960s and 1970s, and the unfortunate necessity for the Me Too movement today, as well as the ongoing silencing of women's voices worldwide and their continuing repression by men. Women still struggle with great inequality in personal relationships, frequently being controlled and silenced in the home, in family life, the workplace. This attitude is reflected in unequal pay scales and in societal attitudes in the wider world. The struggle to be listened to, heard and then taken seriously continues and the issue is far from resolved.

The worship of people

The secularization of society has possibly led to dangerous levels of holding some people as more important than others because there is no "God" for many people these days and perhaps there has to be a replacement if human nature requires it. Social media has helped promote and elevate some individuals above others, leaving the rest feeling "less than." There is huge interest in individuals, with "celebrity," and often for no good reason, except that celebrity culture seeks out and puts them on a pedestal. This approach has spread into the Quaker sphere and Quakers have to beware of raising some individuals above others. The person who is busy, active and talkative is equal to the person who is quiet and takes their place silently in meeting every week, perhaps holding those present in the Light. The tendency to value one over another seems to be hardwired into us and it can lead ultimately to power falling into the wrong hands and the "Devil" coming out to play – with our lives and with the life of the planet.

Margaret Fell herself seems to have revered George Fox above others, at least when she first met him. She, not surprisingly, saw him as a great spiritual leader, possessing almost divine powers and felt him to be different from others. We have to remember that this was possibly a reaction to her own powerful convincement, which must have shaken her to her core and which she attributed to him. Fox was certainly a great leader and healer and did great things, but there were others too. It seems as though Fell wanted to promote him as the founder of Quakerism. She herself became highly revered, in her turn, for her writings, her work, her character, her administration skills and pastoral care and her many other gifts and abilities in the early years of Quakerism. Perhaps we all have tendencies to raise others up to a position of being "more equal" than others.

Equality of ministry

Equality is important, but one which continues to prompt "Yes but ..." We are all children in God and equal in these eyes – or if we are in God and God is in us, then we are all equal in each other's eyes. But what if one of us causes damaging disruption? Should they carry on having their own voice, "being equal"? We are advised that even if ministry is not for us, it might be for someone else. But is it for the rest of us to make judgment calls and curtail behaviors? Or do we put up with the disruption and remain quiet? We have a duty to support others. A person's outpourings may not be given in the spirit of ministry, but come from a deep place of hurt or anger. But what of the spontaneous, outspoken ministry of early Friends – the offence they must have caused? How they were treated – ridiculed, tortured, thrown into prison.

Quaker Elders may feel pressure to discern where ministry comes from in their role in holding the meeting. Who is to say? Who is to decide? Whatever we are uncertain about we have the mechanisms in place, such as discernment in the group, clearness and threshing meetings, for our decision to be made in Truth, and we have to be certain that the ultimate decision comes through Spirit.

True equality in Quakerism?

Is there real equality in Quakerism? The answer? Not yet. Quakers like to think of themselves as treating everyone equally, but we are frequently caught out, or we catch ourselves out, being sexist, racist, transphobic, homophobic, agist – the list is long. Even being aware of equality and having it in our minds fails to save us from the worst kind of pitfall, it seems, even if we have suffered from this on a personal level. As women, we may have been patronized by men over a lifetime, but this does not always teach us to treat everyone equally. It seems to be hard to learn such a lesson. A Friend ministering about a particular problem concerning gender diversity asked us to keep equality uppermost in our minds and think tenderly, in a Quaker way, from a place of love for all.

A question of chairs

Perhaps the relatively recent habit of arranging meetinghouse chairs in a circle, rather than facing in one direction, means that we all face each other as equals, with no one positioned prominently. In meetinghouses that still have the old-style upright wooden benches, an arrangement in an inward-facing oblong works in the same way. Perhaps this practical idea helps us to experience equality in a physical way and gives us a better chance of being able to live out the ideal. The Self and the Other can communicate freely in the equal space of the meeting. This space, or void, can bring us more clarity of belief, thought, followed perhaps by action. Equality can lead to the purity of Truth.

Chapter 4

Peace

We are called to live "in the virtue of that life and power that takes away the occasion of all wars". Do you faithfully maintain our testimony that war and the preparation for war are inconsistent with the spirit of Christ? Search out whatever in your own way of life may contain the seeds of war. Stand firm in our testimony, even when others commit or prepare to commit acts of violence, yet always remember that they too are children of God.

Advices and Queries, number 31

Dear Brethren, Francis Howgill, with the rest with thee who are Prisoners of the Lord, called Faithful and Chosen, abiding Faithful in the will of God, and there stand, you have **Peace**, you have Joy, you have boldness, and you stand over all the World, standing in Righteousness, and there is a pure discerning, springing, which is refresh'd by you.

from *A Brief Collection of Remarkable Passages* (p. 51)

Adaptation

"Friends, and all of you who are imprisoned on behalf of your beliefs, you are faithful and special, having faith in the will of God, so stand in it, rejoice in the peace you find there, live out your joy in it. Feel your boldness and your position in the world as among its leaders in knowing what is right, where there is real discernment and energy, all being added to by you."

Ideas and notes

This piece seems to be advising those going through difficult times (in prison) to take heart and confidence in their faith and experience, in finding a sort of peace in these things. To know that they are doing the right thing in the right way and can contribute to all that is good. Finding peace when you are going through difficulty is hard and it is important to feel encouraged by others. That way peace can grow.

And as the Lord hath loved you with his Everlasting Love, and visited you, and hath made manifest his Eternal Light in you, which is the Way that leads to the Father, and hath raised up the Eternal Witness in you, of his Everlasting Love. So let that Love concern you to love one another, and be serviceable to one another, and that every one may be made willing to suffer for the Body's sake, and that there may be no Rent in the Body, but that the Members have the same Care one over another, and where one Member suffers, all the Members may suffer with it. And here is the Unity of the Spirit, and the Bond of Peace.

from *A Brief Collection of Remarkable Passages* (p. 58)

Adaptation

"And as you are loved in God everlastingly, and been blessed by this love, and have lived out this Light within you, which leads you always towards God, and has made you a witness of this love. Let that love spread so that you love others and are of use to them and they to you. So that we can all be willing to work as parts of a whole, so that there is no weakness in that wholeness, and we all care equally for each other, and so if one person is suffering, we all suffer with them. This is where you find Spirit in unity and the peace which binds you together as a whole."

Ideas and notes

Peace comes about if we work together as a whole, rather than as individuals, and care equally for one another.

Dear Brethren, in the unchangeable, everlasting, powerful Truth of God, my Love salutes you in the Heavenly Union: I am present with you, who are obedient to the measure of the Eternal Light, which never changes, and who abides in the Oneness of the Spirit, and in the Bond of **Peace**, which never can be broken, nor taken from you. Here is Freedom, which the World knows not, to the Measure of God in every particular made manifest, and obeyed, and lived in, doth my Love flow freely to you.

'An Epistle to Friends, that were Prisoners in Lancaster-Castle, by M. Fell, 1654,' from *A Brief Collection of Remarkable Passages* (p. 59)

Adaptation

"Dear Friends, in the unchanging and everlasting love of God, I send my own love: I am with you, all you who follow Light, which never changes, and who remain in Oneness of Spirit, and in peace which unites all, which can never be broken or taken from you. In this there is a particular freedom, which is generally not experienced more broadly, but which is alive in God and made real in it, lived out by you, and my love flows freely to you."

Ideas and notes

Fell continues her thoughts about the love of God bringing peace to all. Inner peace, which brings the group into unity and strength. If we work on inner peace, this spreads out into the world.

* * *

Peace is a feeling, an experience, a resolution. It runs deep within, though it can quickly be swamped by anxious thoughts, worries and negativity. It is a place in the soul where everything stops and stillness is found. It could be the place where that of God lives. Perhaps the peace of stillness can be found in the simplicity of silence. One of our challenges is to access this place of inner peace and then hold on to it, even when jangled thoughts invade – thoughts that can escalate to exasperation, anger, verbal and physical aggression, fighting and then even, eventually, to war-like activity. Perhaps this place of stillness is what Fell is referring to when she uses the word "peace."

On an individual level it is, perhaps, possible to access peace and hold on to it. The danger seems to occur when the individual loses that personal peace and gravitates, instead, towards negative energy, which can take on identity and give an illusion of security. The walls go up. The discontent of many can quickly build up and get out of control, becoming evermore dangerous. Danger can occur too when conflict is suppressed, either individually or in the group, so that outwardly there seems to be peace, while inside there is repressed, unexpressed bad feeling. How can negativity be dispersed safely rather than festering within and surfacing later or differently, perhaps more toxic than before?

Peace Themes

Personal peace

Quakers are well known for their attitudes to peace versus war. And for many this is all they are known for. In her uses of the word "peace," Fell talks about personal, inner peace rather than peace between groups or the anti-war. She asks Friends, particularly those who are struggling, imprisoned and otherwise going through difficult times, to look inside themselves for peace, for the roots of peace, and then live in it and be responsible for it. She asks us to listen to God within, be taught by it and learn from it. She assures us that we will find healing and peace within if we rely on the inward Light in its simplicity. And this is something that we can take for ourselves, and do for ourselves, for today, when all seems sadly jangled and life is a long way from being peaceful – in any sense.

Striving for peace in the world

The Battle of Grosvenor Square, London, which took place in 1968, was part of widespread protest against the Vietnam War and is remembered to this day for its extreme violence and dangerous chaos. I remember police horses rearing on hind legs in the middle of the crowd. In a charged, tense atmosphere anything could have happened. I barely knew why I was there. We had escaped temporarily from our Quaker boarding school, hitch-hiked to London, and it was all a great adventure. On our return, our absence noticed, letters were sent to our parents. These positively acknowledged our anti-war stance and involvement but explained that we would be punished for breaking school rules. The so-called punishment was enlightened. We had to form a pupil committee and arrange a day of speakers, reflecting all sides of the political debate on the Vietnam War, for the whole school to attend. Whether Quaker schools should exist or not is an ongoing discussion for Friends, but this memorable event, including the school's reaction, certainly shaped me.

In many anti-war demonstrations since my teens I have felt the frustration of making a stand but possibly, ultimately, of making no difference. The feeling of solidarity in great numbers is heartening on the day, the shouting of slogans, waving of banners, the youthfulness and camaraderie pull us together and we may make the headlines for a while – and then the mood drifts away and it all seems forgotten or ignored. Nothing seems to take off or go further and another war breaks out somewhere in the world.

War and being war-like seem to be entrenched parts of human nature and there are too many who thirst after it. Being war-like seems hardwired in human nature and it is seen as "normality" or "part of life." Will this ever change? At what point will humanity realize that this model is not working? A sense of powerlessness and the feeling that nothing will ever change renders us small and ineffectual. All we seem to have is the freedom to demonstrate and to hope that we are doing something positive.

Peace spreading out

But perhaps taking part in demonstrations and making personal discoveries in the process are important. This is how you can make peace with yourself and decide how to act, working for a more peaceful world. Personal actions have an impact on how you behave with others and influence them to do good in the world. You can make waves.

A sense of personal peace, being at peace, can spread out to others and the world. A "calm" person can be thanked for spreading calm. They may not necessarily feel the calmness inside, but their demeanor speaks otherwise and they have offered and transmitted peacefulness. They have, perhaps unwittingly, been of service. If we try to "live" peace, this can be part of our ministry. Approaching a volatile situation calmly can dissipate it, even without words being exchanged. The inner tutor instructs us not to react or to only react from a place of peace. Others see that we are not going to anger. They are not going to get a rise out of us. There is not going to be an argument, a fight – and writ large, there will not be a war.

Peace in meeting

Meeting is almost always a place where peace is guaranteed. The feeling has permeated the fabric of the building and is there for all time. It can be counted on. A Friend arriving at meeting feeling upset spoke of finding great peace after the hour was over, even though nothing much seemed to have occurred. Often it seems as though nothing is happening in meeting and that nothing is happening to us. This is more the case if meetings are mostly silent – as they may be these days – people find that there is much to say but nothing emerges as ministry for others. A while after meeting has ended we might revise the thought that nothing much has happened and feel that it seemed that our time was spent in the best way possible. In the following week just the imprinted memory of that peaceful hour may be enough to dispel a bad mood, calm a pointless argument or quieten quelling anxiety – all seeds of war, ultimately.

Meeting may follow a pattern: time being aware of the atmosphere and the quiet of the room and the people in it, noticing the quality of the silence; "worship" – centering down, feeling centered in the Self, wholeness and meaningfulness, perhaps prayer; wondering about the others present and those who are not, how they are and whether they are well, unwell, contented or otherwise; thinking about any ministry; going over problems and to-do lists and wondering how we can stick the hour out. If the weather is good, a restless feeling may worsen. If we are to give notices or introduce an event, then we may think about what we are going to say and how. We may worry about getting information right. In coffee time fellowship and friendship is valuable. Meeting is like extended family – there are people we may know well and others not so well. There are newcomers to greet and get to know. There's a feeling of trust and being able to speak openly without preamble. Loving care, listening and communicating is all there. All this is about working for peace in the individual.

After-effects

During the following week, there is calm and refreshment through simply remembering being in meeting. The effects are long-lasting. Meeting is the place to go to gain peaceful sustenance, belonging and rest as well as community fellowship, action and contribution. Things feel right there and this permeates into other areas of life.

> Friends, and Brethren, in the Eternal Light, Life, and Power of the Eternal Spirit, where our Unity stands, Greeting; Grace and Peace be multiplied amongst you, that in the Unity of the Spirit you may dwell; for they that are joined to the Lord, are one Spirit, and Heart, and one Soul. My dearly Beloved in the Innocency of the Lamb, keep your Station and Habitation, there will you come to read your **Peace**, there will you come to know your Life to come from the Head Jesus Christ, in whom are hid all the Treasures and Riches.
>
> from *A Brief Collection of Remarkable Passages* (p. 98)

Adaptation

"Friends, in the Light, Life and Power of the Spirit, where we are together, Greetings. Let grace and peace spread through you all, so that you can live in Spirit. Those connected in God are one Spirit – heart and soul. Keep to your own place in life, be happy in it, so that there you will find peace, coming to know that your life comes from God, where all the riches of life lie."

Ideas and notes

Fell is saying that peace begins within, in the soul of the individual, and that trying to change and perhaps alter lifestyle, or move out of your original sphere will not bring you greater peace. She is saying be modest and humble, be content where you already are, for that is where true happiness lies. It is easier, too, to find this state when you are with others who are also seeking after the same and trying to live in God.

> Friends and brothers/sisters, in Eternal Light, Life and Power of the Eternal Spirit, where we are united, greeting; let grace and **peace** grow in you, so that you can live in the unity of

the Spirit; for those who are in God are joined in Spirit and heart and together in their very souls. Dearly beloved, in the Lamb's innocence, remain in your own place, where you experience Peace. There you will learn that Life originates in the Light, in which is everything that is of value.

from *A Brief Collection of Remarkable Passages* (p. 97)

Adaptation

"Friends in the light, life and power of the spirit, which holds us together, let grace and peace grow in you, so that you can live in the spirit's unity. Those joined in God are joined in Spirit too. So stay in your own place, where you already have peace. There you will learn that life starts in the Light, and in that place you will find everything that is important in life."

Ideas and notes

The word peace is used here as part of a greeting, and may just be intended as such (peace be with you). However, the idea of peace "growing in you" is a concept that Fell often uses and it puts across the feeling that peace is an effect that gradually takes root in a person and spreads out, first within and then out into other people and the world beyond. Peace is necessary for being in unity with Spirit and with others. She also reiterates the idea of staying where you are in your position in life and finding peace there rather than searching for it elsewhere. We are always searching outside and beyond for what we think is better – perhaps this is part of human nature. The grass is always greener. But we should look within and nurture the peace there first of all in the inward Light.

Therefore Consider this, ye that forget God, lest I tear you in pieces, and there be none to deliver; Now you have Time prize it, this is the Day of your Visitation, wherein the Lord God hath visited you, and called you, and shewed you the way of **Peace**, which shall be an Eternal Witness for the living God against you, if ye rebel against it; for Rebellion is as the Sin of Witchcraft, and Stubbornness, is Iniquity and Idolatry; and if ye reject the word of the Lord, he will also reject you.

from *A Brief Collection of Remarkable Passages* (p. 122)

Adaptation

"Think about this, if you forget that of God, in case I lose patience in my message to you: now you have time, value it. This is the day when you will find God, when you have been pulled towards it and shown where peace lies, which will be a witness for God against you if you fight it and reject it. Rebelling against God is like the sin of doing bad things and being stubborn is like being iniquitous and idolatrous. If you reject God, it will reject you."

Ideas and notes

Fell is resorting to Old Testament language here, with threats and impatience on display. Her words may be strong for our taste.

Therefore in the fear of the Lord God, turn your Minds to within, where the Light shines in the heart, where the Lord teacheth all his People, who are taught of him, are taught by the Light, and guided by the Light, for God is the Light of his Israel; all Children of the Lord, are taught of the Lord, and they are established in righteousness, and they are far from oppression, and great is their **peace**, and the Lord's Children are Taught by the Light.

from *A Brief Collection of Remarkable Passages* (p. 154)

Adaptation

"Therefore, in awe of God, turn within, where the light is shining in your heart, where God teaches us all, who are taught by it learn from it, and are guided by it. For God is Light, all those in God are taught by it and feel goodness spreading out from themselves. They are not oppressed and they experience great peace, and those in God are taught by Light."

Ideas and notes

Peace is to be found inside us all, if we can only learn from the God that is within. This is our teacher and those who can learn from it will find their peace.

> But now is the Lord gathering them that will be gathered, all that do turn unto this witness of God in them, the Lord will heal them. Behold I will bring health, and care, and I will cure them, and will reveal unto them the abundance of **Peace** and Truth.
>
> from *A Brief Collection of Remarkable Passages* (p. 155)

Adaptation

"Now God is affecting those that want to be affected, all those who turn toward that of God within themselves, they will be healed in it. They will be healed, be healthy and will experience Peace and Truth in abundance."

Ideas and notes

That of God comes to those who want it and can turn within and they will find healing and peace.

Concluding Thoughts: Toward Wholeness

Can we ever really reach completeness or "wholeness"? How do you know when you have arrived in that state? I wanted to re-examine Quakerism. I had inherited it, without choice, and I needed to go back to the core of the Light, to see what that really meant for early Friends and what I could learn from it – how I might use it in my own life. It did, indeed, help me to get further along the track toward a kind of wholeness. You can never really say, "I've done it" or "I've got it," but I experience more wholeness in life generally and there are fleeting glimpses of "something." We are all works in progress and will remain in that state forever – still exploring the unknown and the unknowable. In stillness and contemplation, listening always, perhaps we can make partial discoveries. We can live in hope in the Light and, as Fell wrote in her final words: "stand for God and Truth."

> Therefore all turn to the voice that calls ye, this is the way, walk in it: And that which turns and draws your minds towards God, the light which cometh from the father of light turn to, and there will ye witnesse a living hope.
> Margaret Fell

About the Author

Joanna Godfrey Wood has been a Quaker all her life and she attended Quaker school. She recently took the Equipping for Ministry course (two years) at the Woodbrooke Quaker Study Centre in Birmingham, England. This gave her a chance to explore many aspects of Christianity and Quakerism, in the course of which she studied the works of seventeenth-century Quaker Margaret Fell, particularly her writings about the Light. She also looked at the connection between creativity and ministry in a more general way. In her local Quaker meeting her particular ministry is facilitating study groups for local Friends. Joanna spent her working life as a book editor, of both fiction and non-fiction titles. She has also written *Travelling in the Light: How Margaret Fell's writings can speak to Quakers today*, published by The Kindlers, 2019.

Further Reading

Advices and Queries, London: The Yearly Meeting of the Religious Society of Friends (Quakers) in Britain, 2010

Angell, Stephen W. and Dandelion, Pink, *The Cambridge Companion to Quakerism*, Cambridge University Press, 2018

Armstrong, Karen, *The Case for God: what religion really means*, Vintage Books, 2010

Askew Fell Fox, Margaret, *A brief collection of remarkable passages and occurrences relating to the birth, education, life, conversion, travels, services, and deep sufferings of that ancient, eminent, and faithful servant of the Lord, Margaret Fell*, J. Sowle, 1710

Barnett, Craig, *The Guided Life: Finding Purpose in Troubled Times*, Christian Alternative Books, 2019

Barnett, Craig, *Quaker Renewal*, The Friend Publications, 2017

Birkel, Michael, *The Messenger That Goes Before: Reading Margaret Fell for Spiritual Nurture*, Pendle Hill pamphlet 398, Kindle edition, 2017

Boulton, David, *The Trouble with God: Building the Republic of Heaven*, O Books, 2005

Brailsford, M.R., *Quaker Women*, Duckworth, 1915

Brown, David and Rosemary, *Living Adventurously: experiencing Quaker testimonies in Spirit and in the world*, The Kindlers, 2019

Bruyneel, Sally, *Margaret Fell and the End of Time: The Theology of the Mother of Quakerism*, Baylor University Press, 2010

Crosfield, Helen G., *Margaret Fox of Swarthmoor Hall*, Headley Brothers, 1913

Dandelion, Ben Pink, *Open for Transformation*, Quaker Books, 2014

Fox, Matthew, *Original Blessing*, Bear & Co, 1983

Gill, Catie and Hobby, Elaine, *This I Warn You in Love: witness of some early Quaker women*, The Kindlers, 2013

Gline, Elsa F., *Undaunted Zeal: The Letters of Margaret Fell*, Friends United Press, 2003

Godfrey Wood, Joanna, *Travelling in the Light: how Margaret Fell's writings can speak to Quakers today*, The Kindlers, 2019

Guiton, Derek, *A Man that Looks on Glass: standing up for God in the Religious Society of Friends (Quakers)*, FeedARead Publishing, 2015

Guiton, Derek, *The Beyond Within*, FeedARead Publishing, 2017

Kelly, Thomas, *A Testament of Devotion*, Harper and Bros, 1941

Kunz, Bonnelyn Young, *Margaret Fell and the Rise of Quakerism*, Stanford University Press, 1993

Martin, Marcelle, *Our Life is Love: The Quaker Spiritual Journey*, Inner Light Books, 2016

Muers, Rachel, *Testimony: Quakerism and Theological Ethics*, 2015, SCM Press

Nickalls, John L. (ed.), *The Journal of George Fox*, Philadelphia Religious Society of Friends and Quaker Books Britain Yearly Meeting, 2005

Post Abbott, Margery, *To Be Broken and Tender: A Quaker Theology for Today*, Kindle edition, 2016

Post Abbott, Margery, *Walk Humbly, Serve Boldly: Modern Quakers as Everyday Prophets*, Inner Light Books, 2018

Punshon, John, *Portrait in Grey: A Short History of the Quakers*, Quaker Home Service, 1984

Quaker Faith and Practice: The book of Christian discipline of the Yearly Meeting of the Religious Society of Friends (Quakers) in Britain, 1994

Ross, Isabel, *Margaret Fell: Mother of Quakerism*, William Sessions Ltd, 1996

Rowlands, Helen (ed.), *God, Words and Us: Quakers in conversation about religious difference*, Quaker Books, 2017

Sharman, Cecil, *George Fox and the Quakers*, Quaker Books, 1991

Soelle, Dorothee, *The Silent Cry: Mysticism and Resistance*, Fortress Press, 2001

Trevett, Christine, *Women and Quakerism in the Seventeenth Century*, William Sessions Ltd, 1992

Also in this series

Quaker Roots and Branches
John Lampen

Quaker Roots and Branches explores what Quakers call their
'testimonies' – the interaction of inspiration, faith and action to
bring change in the world. It looks at Quaker concerns around
the sustainability of the planet, peace and war, punishment,
and music and the arts in the past and today. It stresses the
continuity of their witness over three hundred and sixty-five
years as well as their openness to change and development.

Telling the Truth about God
Rhiannon Grant

Telling the truth about God without excluding anyone is a
challenge to the Quaker community. Drawing on the author's
academic research into Quaker uses of religious language and
her teaching to Quaker and academic groups, Rhiannon Grant
aims to make accessible some key theological and philosophical
insights. She explains that Quakers might sound vague but are
actually making clear and creative theological claims.

What Do Quakers Believe?
Geoffrey Durham

Geoffrey Durham answers the crucial question 'What do
Quakers believe?' clearly, straightforwardly and without
jargon. In the process he introduces a unique religious group
whose impact and influence in the world is far greater than
their numbers suggest. *What Do Quakers Believe?* is a friendly,
direct and accessible toe-in-the-water book for readers who
have often wondered who these Quakers are, but have never
quite found out.

CHRISTIAN ALTERNATIVE
BOOKS

THE NEW OPEN SPACES

Throughout the two thousand years of Christian tradition there have been, and still are, groups and individuals that exist in the margins and upon the edge of faith. But in Christianity's contrapuntal history it has often been these outcasts and pioneers that have forged contemporary orthodoxy out of former radicalism as belief evolves to engage with and encompass the ever-changing social and scientific realities. Real faith lies not in the comfortable certainties of the Orthodox, but somewhere in a half-glimpsed hinterland on the dirt track to Emmaus, where the Death of God meets the Resurrection, where the supernatural Christ meets the historical Jesus, and where the revolution liberates both the oppressed and the oppressors.

Welcome to Christian Alternative... a space at the edge where the light shines through.
If you have enjoyed this book, why not tell other readers by posting a review on your preferred book site.

Recent bestsellers from Christian Alternative are:

Bread Not Stones
The Autobiography of An Eventful Life
Una Kroll
The spiritual autobiography of a truly remarkable woman and a history of the struggle for ordination in the Church of England.
Paperback: 978-1-78279-804-0 ebook: 978-1-78279-805-7

The Quaker Way
A Rediscovery
Rex Ambler
Although fairly well known, Quakerism is not well understood.
The purpose of this book is to explain how Quakerism works as
a spiritual practice.
Paperback: 978-1-78099-657-8 ebook: 978-1-78099-658-5

Blue Sky God
The Evolution of Science and Christianity
Don MacGregor
Quantum consciousness, morphic fields and blue-sky
thinking about God and Jesus the Christ.
Paperback: 978-1-84694-937-1 ebook: 978-1-84694-938-8

Celtic Wheel of the Year
Tess Ward
An original and inspiring selection of prayers combining
Christian and Celtic Pagan traditions, and interweaving their
calendars into a single pattern of prayer for every morning
and night of the year.
Paperback: 978-1-90504-795-6

Christian Atheist
Belonging without Believing
Brian Mountford
Christian Atheists don't believe in God but miss him: especially
the transcendent beauty of his music, language, ethics, and
community.
Paperback: 978-1-84694-439-0 ebook: 978-1-84694-929-6

Compassion Or Apocalypse?
A Comprehensible Guide to the Thoughts of René Girard
James Warren
How René Girard changes the way we think about God and the
Bible, and its relevance for our apocalypse-threatened world.
Paperback: 978-1-78279-073-0 ebook: 978-1-78279-072-3

Diary Of A Gay Priest
The Tightrope Walker
Rev. Dr. Malcolm Johnson
Full of anecdotes and amusing stories, but the Church is still a
dangerous place for a gay priest.
Paperback: 978-1-78279-002-0 ebook: 978-1-78099-999-9

Do You Need God?
Exploring Different Paths to Spirituality Even For Atheists
Rory J.Q. Barnes
An unbiased guide to the building blocks of spiritual belief.
Paperback: 978-1-78279-380-9 ebook: 978-1-78279-379-3

Readers of ebooks can buy or view any of these bestsellers by
clicking on the live link in the title. Most titles are published
in paperback and as an ebook. Paperbacks are available in
traditional bookshops. Both print and ebook formats are
available online.

Find more titles and sign up to our readers' newsletter at
http://www.johnhuntpublishing.com/christianity
Follow us on Facebook at
https://www.facebook.com/ChristianAlternative